Japan

Japan

BY ANN HEINRICHS

Enchantment of the World
Second Series

Children's Press®
A Division of Grolier Publishing

NEW YORK   LONDON   HONG KONG   SYDNEY

DANBURY, CONNECTICUT

Consultant: Yoshiko Yokochi Samuel, Professor, Wesleyan University, Middletown, Connecticut

Please note: All statistics are as up-to-date as possible at the time of publication.

Visit Children's Press on the Internet: http://publishing.grolier.com
Book Production by Editorial Directions, Inc.
Book Design by Ox and Company

Library of Congress Cataloging-in-Publication Data

Heinrichs, Ann.

　　　　Japan / by Ann Heinrichs.

　　　　p. cm. — (Enchantment of the world. Second series)

　　　　Includes bibliographical references and index.
Summary: Describes the history and culture of the island nation of Japan.
　　　　ISBN 0-516-20649-4
　　　　1. Japan—Juvenile literature. [1. Japan.] I. Title. II. Series
　　　　DS806.H35　1998
　　　　952—dc21   97-38771
　　　　　　　　　　　　　　　　　　　　　　　　　　　　　　　CIP
　　　　　　　　　　　　　　　　　　　　　　　　　　　　　　　AC

Acknowledgments

I am grateful to employees of the Consulate General of Japan and the Japan National Tourism Office for their kind assistance in this project, and to the many Japanese people who shared their visions and memories with me.

Contents

Cover photo:
Japanese schoolgirls

Central Hokkaido

Inventing the New Japan

Twelve-year-old Keiko shoulders her backpack, smooths her navy-blue uniform, and dashes off to catch the 7 A.M. train. The hour-long trip to school gives her a chance to look over her homework for the day.

AFTER SEVEN HOURS OF CLASS WORK
and another train ride, Keiko's back at
home. Now she has less than an hour to
ride her bike, call her friends, or read her
superheroine comics. Then it's time for
three hours of *juku,* or "cram school."

Keiko has been in juku for four years
already. These intense, after-school classes
will help her to score well on entrance
exams for high school and, later, college.
This, in turn, will assure her of a good job
as a research biologist.

High school boys at the Nijo
Castle in Kyoto

Keiko's neighbor Yoshio doesn't attend juku. After school,
he has time to practice guitar, watch videos, and play with his
massive array of computer games. Now fifteen, Yoshio knows
he'll soon have to buckle down and study for college exams.
But for now, he just wants to have a good time.

Both Keiko and Yoshio are examples of Japan's changing
society. Keiko follows the traditional Japanese work ethic,
which starts as early as kindergarten. What's new is that Keiko
is a girl. In her mother's time, most girls expected to become
homemakers rather than professional career women.

Opposite: **Young students
visit the Golden Pavilion.**

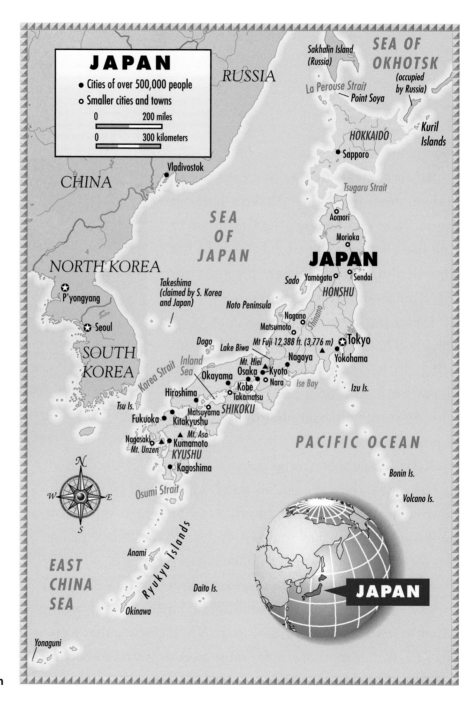

Geopolitical map of Japan

Yoshio will pass through the same school system as Keiko, but if his test scores are low, he still has more choices than his parents had. He might go to work for a small, offbeat computer-software firm rather than a large corporation. Then, with no nighttime business dinners to attend, he'd be free to hang out in karaoke clubs with his friends.

Keiko and Yoshio live in a different world from the one their parents and grandparents knew. For the older generation, growing up in the 1940s was a nightmare. They saw their country reduced to rubble in World War II. Hungry people scoured the countryside for food, many of them in ragged clothes and bare feet.

What kept them going? For many, it was *taeru*—a deeply ingrained virtue of Japan's famed warriors. Emperor Hirohito once explained the term. "Taeru," he said, "is to bear the unbearable."

After the war, haunted by their memories, people worked slavishly to make a better life for their families. This work ethic brought about an "economic miracle." In just a few years, Japan became one of the wealthiest, most productive countries in the world. The same ethic created Japan's high-pressure education system.

Growing up in modern Japan is nothing like growing up during the war. Children in Japan today have clothes, toys, and leisure time. When a Japanese ad agency asked teenagers what they wanted most in life, they said they wanted their own room, their own phone, and their own boyfriend or girlfriend. Fifty years earlier, a teenager might have hoped for a heaping bowl of rice.

Downtown Osaka

But traditional values of duty and honor are far from dying out. A recent government survey found that young adults in Japan want to contribute to society. They're also concerned about environmental problems and international cooperation.

Steeped in tradition, battered by war, Japan reinvented itself as a high-tech nation. Now, with a fresh vision, Japan is inventing yet another identity for itself in the twenty-first century.

Islands Born from the Sea

An ancient Japanese legend tells how Japan began. From their heavenly home, Izanagi and Izanami spied the speck we call Earth. To see what it was like, they descended the Floating Bridge to Heaven. Izanagi thrust his jeweled spear into the sea, drew it out, and gave it a shake. A drop of brine fell away and became Onogoro, Japan's first island. After that, Izanagi and Izanami had many children. Each was an island of Japan.

The Inland Sea of Japan

Land of the Rising Sun

JAPAN'S LEGENDARY ANCESTORS WERE FERTILE INDEED. THEY spawned more than 3,900 islands. This archipelago, or string of islands, gently curves around northeast Asia's mainland for about 1,200 miles (1,930 km). Added together, the islands cover almost as much land as California in the United States.

The four main islands, from the largest on down, are Honshu, Hokkaido, Kyushu, and Shikoku. They make up more than 95 percent of Japan's land area. Smaller islands are the tips of underwater mountains.

Japan's east coast greets the sunrise across the Pacific Ocean. *Nippon*, the nation's Japanese name, means "land of the rising sun." To the west, across the Sea of Japan, are Russia and North and South Korea. China lies to the southwest, beyond the East China Sea. On the north, Japan faces the Sea of Okhotsk and Russia's Sakhalin and Kuril islands.

Japan belongs not only to Asia, but also to the Pacific Rim—a great circle of lands bordering the Pacific Ocean. The Philippines, Indonesia, Australia, Chile, California, and Alaska are also part of the Pacific Rim. They share many geological features, as well as trade ties.

Previous page: **Aerial view of the Kuril Islands**

Fuji-san

Mount Fuji, also known as Fuji-san or Fujiyama, is the sacred mountain of the ancient Shinto fire goddess. More than a million people climb Fuji every year during the official climbing season of July and August. Fuji is 12,388 feet (3,776 m) high, and its crater has a diameter of about 1,650 feet (503 m). It last erupted in 1707.

Mountains and Plains

Japan's landscape is rugged and wild, with jagged mountains and steep, forested hills. Mountain ranges run like a backbone down the length of the country. They divide Japan into its outer and inner zones. The outer zone, which faces out toward the Pacific Ocean, is uneven, cut by many inlets and bays. This area gets the brunt of tidal waves and typhoons. The inner zone, west of the mountains, faces the Sea of Japan.

Japan's highest mountain ranges are the Japanese Alps, in the central part of Honshu Island. Closer to the Pacific coast is

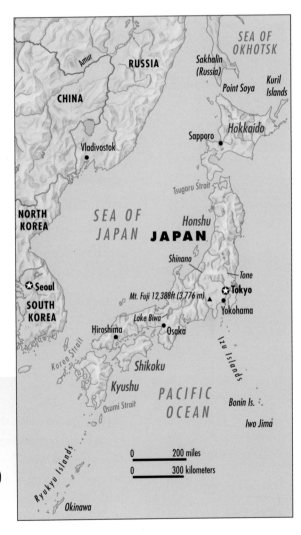

Geographical Features

Area: 145,870 square miles (377,802 sq km)

Highest Elevation: Mount Fuji, 12,388 feet (3,776 m)

Lowest Elevation: Sea level along coasts

Longest River: Shinano (on Honshu), 228 miles (367 km)

Largest City: Tokyo

Average Annual Precipitation: 40 inches (102 cm)

Skiing the snow-covered Alps

Mount Fuji, Japan's highest peak and at one time an active volcano. Falling volcanic ash gave the mountain its cone shape. Fuji is snowcapped almost all year round. On clear days, people can see it from Tokyo, about 70 miles (113 km) away.

Broad, flat plains lie between the mountain ridges that run down to the coast. Cities, industries, and farms are located on these plains. Only a small portion of Japan's lands can be farmed. Most agriculture takes place on the coastal plains, but farmers also cultivate the basins and valleys between the mountains.

Island by Island

The northern island of Hokkaido is hilly and cool, with harsh winters. About 5 percent of Japan's population lives here, including the Ainu people, a native ethnic minority. Hokkaido is a popular spot for skiing and other winter sports, and national parks cover much of the island's interior. The rolling hills of Ishikari Plain are the best farming region. Sapporo is Hokkaido's major city.

Sapporo

Sapporo gained international fame when it hosted the 1972 Winter Olympics. The city is one of the most modern in Japan, with a neatly laid out city plan. Because the winters are so cold, there are underground shopping malls. Trees and flowers line O-dori, the main boulevard. During the world-famous Snow Festival in February, the city is filled with gigantic ice carvings, such as the castle ice sculpture shown at left. Other attractions are the botanical gardens, the Ainu Museum, and the Sapporo brewery.

Yokohama

Yokohama is Japan's second-largest city and its major port. In the 1850s, the first Western traders in Japan were allowed to settle in Yokohama. It quickly grew from a fishing village to a large commercial port. The 1923 earthquake and the bombs of World War II destroyed much of the city, but many historic structures remain. Among them are two important temples, Sojiji and Gumyoji, and Sankei-en Garden's pagodas and villas. Chinatown and the Silk Museum, both near Yamashita Park, add to Yokohama's cultural interest.

Nagoya

With more than 2 million residents, Nagoya is Japan's fourth-largest city. Once a way station along the ancient Tokyo-Kyoto Road, it's now a busy international port and manufacturing center. Visitors can view the historic surroundings from the 590-foot (180-m) Television Tower. Nagoya Castle was built by the ruler Tokugawa Ieyasu in 1610. Destroyed in World War II, it has been faithfully rebuilt. The Tokugawa Museum of Art preserves family treasures, including scroll paintings for *The Tale of Genji*. Atsuta Shrine is one of the most important in Japan. On the city's outskirts stands Inuyama Castle, built in 1440, the oldest castle in the country.

Honshu, Japan's largest island, comprises about three-fifths of the nation's land area. Most of Japan's people live there. Northern Honshu is a rich farming region. Sendai, on the east coast, is the major city in the north. Rice fields cover the broad Sendai Plain. Across the mountains, near the Sea of Japan, winters are cold and snowy.

The Kanto Plain, in east-central Honshu, is the major center of population, farming, and industry. Tokyo, the capital, and Yokohama are the largest cities in the Kanto district. The two flow together as one metropolitan area around Tokyo Bay.

Osaka

Japan's third-largest city, Osaka, is the industrial center for the western part of the country. It lies in the Yodo River Delta, where hundreds of bridges span the streams that flow into Osaka Bay. Almost half of Japan's foreign trade goes through the port of Osaka. Modern skyscrapers serve the business and shopping districts. On the traditional side, Osaka is the place to see *bunraku* (puppet) theater. Osaka Castle is a reconstructed version of an earlier castle built by the shogun Tokugawa Ieyasu.

Farther down the Pacific Coast is the Tokai region. Its major city is Nagoya, on the Nobi Plain at the head of Ise Bay. Tokai is especially known as a tea-producing region.

Osaka, Kyoto, and Kobe are the dominant cities on the Kinki Plain of southern Honshu. They, too, form a continuous metropolitan area. Okayama and Hiroshima are also important cities in the south.

Shikoku Island fits into a niche of southern Honshu. The waterway between the two islands, called the Inland Sea, is more like a river, with heavy "traffic" between the two banks. On Shikoku's north bank stand the cities of Takamatsu and Matsuyama.

Bridges and tunnels across the narrow Kammon Strait connect Kyushu Island and Honshu. Like Honshu, Kyushu is heavily populated and highly industrialized. Northern Kyushu is a center for heavy manufacturing, based on coal and steel industries. Fukuoka and Kitakyushu are important cities in this area.

Nagasaki and Sasebo, on Kyushu's west coast, are longtime shipbuilding centers. Kyushu is called "Silicon Island" because

Kyoto

Emperor Kammu founded Kyoto in 794, and the city remained Japan's imperial capital for more than 1,000 years. It was also the nation's cultural and artistic center. Today, Kyoto is Japan's seventh-largest city, with 1.4 million people. It is a center for the textile industry, as well as a religious center. Kyoto has more than 1,600 Buddhist temples and 270 Shinto shrines, including Ginkakuji (Temple of the Silver Pavilion) and the golden-walled Kinkakuji (Temple of the Golden Pavilion). Momoyama Castle was built by the sixteenth-century ruler Toyotomi Hideyoshi. Kyoto National Museum houses more than 10,000 artworks. The Heian Shrine, a replica of Emperor Kammu's imperial palace, was built in 1895 for the 1,100th anniversary of Kyoto's founding.

Congested Kyushu Island

of the semiconductor industries around Kumamoto. Active volcanoes and *onsen* (steaming-hot mineral springs) are among Kyushu's other features.

Moon Beach at Okinawa

The Ryukyu, Bonin, and Kuril Islands

In the south, the Ryukyu Islands curve around to the southwest toward the island nation of Taiwan. In fact, a person can see the mountains of Taiwan from Yonaguni, the last island in the chain.

Okinawa, the major island in the Ryukyus, is a tropical paradise with its white-sand beaches, coral reefs, and lush jungle foliage. Sugarcane production and tourism are the island's main economic activities. The United States occupied Okinawa during World War II. Only in 1972 was it returned to Japan, although the United States keeps military bases there.

The volcanic Bonin Islands trace a southeasterly line out from central Honshu. Minamitori Island, Japan's easternmost point, lies far out in the Pacific Ocean.

The four little Kuril Islands, northeast of Hokkaido, are disputed territory. Japan claims them, but Russia occupies them.

Rivers and Lakes

Japan's rivers are short, swift streams. Some become spectacular waterfalls as they plunge down sheer mountainsides, while others wind through breathtaking mountain gorges. For the adventurous, shooting the whitewater rapids is a thrilling kayak ride. The

Kiso, Hozu, Tneryu, and Kuma Rivers are known for their rapids. Fantastic gorges line the Kurobe, Soun, and Takachiho rivers.

Though they are not suitable for navigation, Japan's rivers provide irrigation for crops and hydroelectric power. Heavy rain and melting snow sometimes swell the rivers until they flood their banks.

Many of Japan's lakes are set amid gorgeous mountain scenery, their glassy surfaces reflecting snowy peaks. Some, such as the Five Fuji Lakes, were formed when volcanic lava dammed a river. Others are the rain-filled craters of inactive volcanoes. Lakes Towada and Tazawa (Japan's deepest) are crater lakes in northern Honshu. Lakes in the mountains are wonderfully clean and clear—Lake Mashu is said to be the clearest lake in the world. The largest of Japan's many lakes is Biwa, near Kyoto.

Thousands of years ago, the Sea of Japan was a lake, too. When more ocean water was frozen in polar ice caps, the sea level was lower than it is today. Two land bridges, now under-water, connected Japan to the Asian mainland. One bridge was attached to Siberia, and the other joined the Korean Peninsula. In between was the lake that is now the Sea of Japan.

Violent Beginnings, Natural Disasters

Japan gets more than its share of natural disasters. Earthquakes, volcanoes, and tidal waves ravage the country every year. A little geological history helps to explain these events.

Japan sits at the meeting place of four tectonic plates, or shifting sections of the Earth's crust. Millions of years ago, the plates smashed together. As the crust buckled and warped,

Mount Unzen on Kyushu spews volcanic ash into the air.

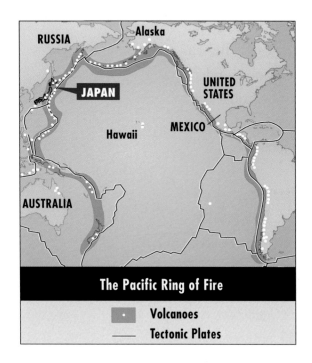

The Pacific Ring of Fire

· Volcanoes
— Tectonic Plates

Japan rose up out of the sea. The intense pressure created enough heat to melt the Earth's rocky crust. Volcanoes erupted, spewing out ash and molten rock and adding more bulk to Japan's craggy surface.

Deep ocean trenches lie off Japan's east coast. These are the places where tectonic plates meet and continue to rub and smash against one another. It is this friction that causes Japan's most violent phenomena: volcanoes, earthquakes, and tidal waves.

The Ring of Fire

Japan has more than 250 volcanoes, and dozens of them are active. They're part of the Pacific region's Ring of Fire. Other volcanoes around this ring are Indonesia's Krakatoa, Washington State's Mount St. Helens, and Alaska's Mount Wrangell.

The most active volcanoes are on southern Hokkaido, northern Honshu, central Honshu near Mount Fuji, and Kyushu Island. Mount Unzen, on western Kyushu, killed more than thirty people when it erupted in 1991. Fifteen thousand people died in its 1792 eruption. Kyushu's Mount Aso is the largest volcano in the world. Its crater is so big that several villages are scattered inside it.

Earthquakes and Tsunamis

According to Japanese folklore, earthquakes happen when catfish flap their tails. There's also a belief that disastrous earthquakes come every seventy years.

The Kanto earthquake of 1923 was Japan's worst in the twentieth century. It killed 143,000 people in the Tokyo-Yokohama area. As the seventy-year point drew near, many Japanese were nervously eyeing the catfish. And the predictions weren't too far off. The Kobe earthquake of 1995 was the worst in recent history.

About 1,500 earthquakes affect Japan every year. Not one day passes without at least a slight tremor somewhere in the country. Students in Japanese schools regularly have earthquake drills to prepare for these disasters. They learn to stay calm, move in an orderly way, and protect themselves from injury.

Japan has elaborate, high-tech systems for predicting earthquakes. Unfortunately, they're not always reliable. Some scientists believe that animals really do give telltale signs. Days before the Kobe disaster, for example, schools of deep-water fish were swimming unusually close to the surface. And on the morning of the quake, flocks of crows began squawking madly and flying in bizarre patterns.

Monstrous ocean waves called *tsunamis* often come with earthquakes. Sometimes called "tidal waves," tsunamis really have nothing to do with the tides. Underwater volcanoes or offshore earthquakes start them in motion. By the time they crash against the coast, they may be moving 100 miles (161 km) an hour.

The Kobe Earthquake

The tremor began on January 17, 1995, at 5:46 in the morning and lasted less than a minute. Yet this earthquake was Japan's worst disaster since World War II. Toppled buildings, twisted highways, and raging fires left 5,500 people dead and thousands injured. Many of the dead were crushed inside their homes. Some lived in wooden houses that had heavy tile roofs built to withstand typhoons, but the roofs caved in when the Earth shook.

Climate

Suppose you could slide Japan directly east around the globe. It would line up perfectly along the eastern seaboard of the United States. Northern Hokkaido would overlap the state of Maine, and in the south, the Ryukyu Islands would match up with the Florida Keys. This gives you an idea of what Japan's climate is like.

Like the east coast of the United States, Japan has a mild, moist climate. In the far north, as in Maine, summers are cool and winters are bitterly cold. The far south is subtropical all year round.

Ocean currents keep Japan's seacoast from being either too hot or too cold. One warm current sweeps up along the south and east coasts as far as Tokyo. Another current swirls into the Sea of Japan, warming the winter air and changing it to heavy snow. Honshu's northwest coast is known as "snow country." Its snowfall is so heavy that roofs may collapse under the weight of the snow. The Pacific Coast, on the other hand, is windy and cold in winter but dry.

From Cherry Blossoms to Golden Leaves

Spring is the most pleasant time of year. The Japanese mark the coming of spring with *sakura zensen*—the cherry-blossom front. In February, weather forecasters start announcing when and where the cherry trees will bloom. The first blossoms open in the south in late March. Then, week by week, the cherry-blossom front moves farther north. Hokkaido's cherries bloom in mid-May.

Summer begins and ends with rainy seasons. The *baiu* (plum rains), which last for a month, begin in early June in the south and move north. On Kyushu Island, this is the heaviest rainfall of the year. Next come the hot, humid days of midsummer. In late August, the *shurin* rainy season begins and lasts through September.

September is typhoon season, too. (The word *typhoon* comes from the Japanese word *taifu*, meaning "wind that blows over Taiwan and toward China.") Like hurricanes, typhoons begin over the ocean, gathering strength and speed. When they hit land, their high winds and violent rains uproot trees and houses. Japan gets about three or four typhoons per season.

By October, the air is cool and crisp, and the mountainsides are ablaze with the red and gold of changing leaves. Japan's autumn is short, as winter begins in November. Hokkaido's winters are the coldest in the country. Asahikawa, on Hokkaido, registered Japan's lowest-ever temperature of –42°F (–41°C). By late February, warmer air drifts in, paving the way for another cherry-blossom spring.

Picturesque agricultural fields and mountains of central Hokkaido

Treasures of Nature

In Tokyo, people can rent dogs or cats by the week or just for a few hours. One shop rents exotic pets such as raccoons and armadillos. Others sell toy pets made of paper, plastic, or wood.

Love of animals is a deep-seated tradition among the Japanese. In folklore, animals are revered as protectors, mischief makers, or messengers of the gods. Frogs and cranes are favorite figures in *origami*, the traditional Japanese art of paper-folding. Plants hold a special place in Japanese culture, too. Chrysanthemums, twisted pines, and blossoming trees have appeared in Japanese art for hundreds of years.

Forests cover more than 60 percent of Japan. Oak, birch, maple, elm, beech, and poplar trees cover the hillsides in central Honshu. In springtime, wildflowers carpet these hillsides, while cherry and plum trees are in bloom.

In the north are conifers, or cone-bearing evergreens—cypress, cedar, spruce, pine, and fir. Only conifers can survive at the highest elevations. On cold, rocky mountain ridges, they grow in eerie, twisted shapes.

Toward the south, the sago palm, camphor tree, bamboo, and wild fig flourish. Broad-leaved evergreens grow on the Ryukyu Islands, and mangrove swamps line the coasts.

National Flowers of Japan

Japan has three national flowers. The chrysanthemum is the emblem of the emperor. It appears on his crest, and he sits on the Chrysanthemum Throne. The plum blossom is considered the first sign of spring. The cherry blossom (above) is a traditional national symbol.

Opposite: **Japanese gardens are among the most beautiful in the world.**

Japanese Wood Folklore

cedar	Carrying a cedar cane will help you reach your goals.
chestnut	Eating with chestnut chopsticks for a year will make you a millionaire.
cypress	Symbolizes hope. Its Japanese name means "tomorrow it will happen."
gingko	Hanging a gingko ornament from the waist keeps colds away.
pine	Symbolizes a long and harmonious life.
plum	Biting on a young plum branch cures a toothache.
zelkova	Burning this wood keeps mice away for two years.

Antelope, deer, and wild boar run free in Japan's remote mountain areas. The forests shelter foxes, squirrels, rabbits, and mice. Many of these species crossed a now-sunken land bridge from China. The delicate shika deer is native to Japan. Thought to be divine messengers, the deer range freely on temple grounds and in national parks.

Brown bears live mainly on Hokkaido, where they are considered sacred by the Ainu people. Asiatic black bears are now endangered in Japan and throughout Asia. (In China, they're hunted for their gallbladders, which are used in traditional medicine.)

Macaques, or snow monkeys, are the fabled characters who "see no evil, hear no evil, and speak no evil." The macaques of northern Honshu live farther north than any other monkey in the world. In wintertime, they love to warm up in steaming hot springs. When they scamper out, icicles droop from their fur.

As more forests are cut, macaques are losing their natural homes. To get food,

they raid orchards and farms. In some cases, macaques have wiped out farmers' entire crops. Farmers trap or shoot the macaques, but more hungry monkeys soon replace them. Scientists are working on ways to control the macaques without killing them.

Japanese folklore is full of tales about the *tanuki*, or raccoon dog. This crafty forest animal is a member of the dog family, but it looks more like a fox with a raccoon's face. According to legend, tanukis dance in the moonlight, change into handsome young men, or drink too much rice wine. Statues of the lighthearted tanuki—with a big smile, an account book, and a jug of wine—are fondly displayed in gardens and shops.

Japanese macaques bathing in the hot springs

Another forest animal, the fox, is honored in Shinto mythology. Shrines for Inari, the fox god, are found throughout the country. Inari is a cunning messenger of the gods, so people seek his help in making shrewd business decisions. They offer his favorite foods—fried soybean curd and rice—at his shrines.

Birds and Fish

Pheasants and snow grouse graze the forest floor for insects and seeds. Other forest birds are green woodpeckers, spotted woodpeckers, Eurasian jays, brown-eared bulbuls, and golden thrushes.

Herons, swans, ducks, and cranes nest and fish along riverbanks. Near the coasts, white-tailed eagles and black kites swoop down to snatch fish from the water. Kites are striking figures, gliding on a wingspan of 5 feet (1.5 m). The rare East Asian ibis and black-billed stork are protected by law.

"Wan, wan!"

The Japanese word for a dog's barking sound is *wan* instead of *woof*. Dog lovers in Japan even have a magazine called *Wan*.

The Tibetan shih tzu breed is a popular small dog. People who have room for a large dog might keep a bulldog or a husky. Some dogs carry little backpacks on their backs with their brushes, snacks, and towels. In pet salons, doggie hairdos cost from $60 to over $150.

Boggy and May's is a pet restaurant in Tokyo. (No, they do not cook pets!) It's a restaurant where pets and their owners can dine together. The pet menu includes both low-calorie dishes and treats.

The National Bird

The *tancho*, or red-crowned crane, is Japan's national bird. It is the largest of the world's fifteen crane species. And in Japanese art, it is a symbol of good fortune and long life. The tancho performs an eerie dance. It bows its graceful neck, arches its back, and springs several feet into the air.

In past centuries, the tancho lived throughout much of Honshu. By the 1800s, hunters had cleared these beautiful birds from the island. Today, only about 600 remain in Japan. They live in the marshes of Hokkaido, feeding on fish, insects, and grain. Killing them is now against the law, but their wetland homes are in danger of being drained and filled for farmland.

Sparrows, swallows, pigeons, and bulbuls are familiar city birds, and big-city garbage also attracts owls and crows. In Tokyo, jungle crows have become a terrible nuisance. These noisy, pushy pests dive at pedestrians and rip garbage bags apart.

Sardines, tuna, mackerel, and sea bream are warm-water fish found in Japan's southern waters. Coral reefs off the southern islands harbor dazzling tropical fish. The colder northern waters are home to salmon, herring, cod, halibut, and crab. Carp are plentiful in rivers and lakes. The Japanese have also farm-raised them for more than 300 years.

Environmental Protection

Japan's industries expanded wildly after World War II. This led to serious air and water pollution in the 1950s and 1960s. Along with the pollution came health problems. Factory wastes in the waters off Kyushu Island caused Minamata disease, or mercury poisoning. Other wastes caused cadmium and arsenic poisoning. Air pollution led to respiratory diseases in tens of thousands of people.

Finally, angry citizens demanded that the government take action. Basic antipollution laws were passed in 1967, and the Environmental Agency was established in 1971. Since then, the government has spent billions of dollars to cut pollution. Industries are required to join the battle, too. Steelmakers have cut the amount of carbon dioxide they release into the air. And many industries have developed bioremediation, which uses tiny organisms to break up pollutants.

Since the 1950s, Japan's forests have been heavily cut for lumber. Mountainsides are stripped, leading to erosion and landslides, and forest animals lose their homes. Today, there are reforestation programs to plant new trees in cleared areas, but in many places, the trees are cut down faster than they can regrow.

Several environmental groups are active in Japan today. Some work with the government to study water conditions, as well as animal and plant life.

Factories pollute the air over Fuji.

Chronicles of a Nation

Japanese legend tells us that the first emperor was Jimmu Tenno, great-great-great-grandson of the sun goddess Amaterasu. It's said that he started the Yamato dynasty, or ruling family, in 660 B.C.

At this point, legend joins with fact. Japan's first known rulers were tribal chiefs on the Yamato Plains of southern Honshu. According to historians, Jimmu, whose name means "divine warrior," most likely ruled in the first century A.D.

This clay figure is from the Jomon culture in Japan, about 350–250 B.C.

THE ORIGINAL INHABITANTS OF JAPAN ARRIVED OVER 10,000 years ago, migrating from the Asian mainland. Their homes were caves or pit houses, built partly underground.

As early as 5000 B.C., pottery-making people of the Jomon culture lived in Japan. Around 300 B.C., a period called the Yayoi, a rice-farming people arrived. Some scholars believe that it was the people of this period who are the ancestors of today's Japanese people. They settled in scattered farming villages, intermarried, and developed a distinct language. Within 300 to 400 years, they looked and spoke much as Japanese people do today.

The chief of each *uji*, or clan, had his own band of warriors. The local religion was an early form of Shinto. People honored creator gods, spirits in nature, and the spirits of their ancestors. Each clan had its own tribal gods, too, and a shaman who communicated with them.

The Yamatos

Around A.D. 300, Yamato chiefs began conquering neighboring tribes. By the fifth century, the Yamatos even ruled part of Korea, on the Asian mainland.

Opposite: **A statue of a samurai warrior guards the Imperial Palace in Tokyo.**

The Yamatos' royal court had friendly relations with Korea, however. Korean immigrants brought their art and metalworking skills with them and introduced Chinese culture to Japan. In the fifth and sixth centuries, visitors brought the Chinese writing system, the teachings of the Chinese philosopher Confucius, and the Buddhist religion.

The Yamato prince Shotoku welcomed these imports. He adopted the Chinese calendar and the Chinese system of government. His constitution of A.D. 604 embraced both Confucian and Buddhist principles.

Shotoku became a faithful follower of Buddhism. As a sign of his faith, he built many Buddhist temples. In 607, he built Horyuji Temple near Nara, where it stands today—Japan's oldest temple.

The Taika Reforms

Until this time, Japan had been a loose society of clans and villages. Under the Taika Reform Edict of 646, Japan was organized into provinces under a central government. The land was divided into strips and squares, which made it easier to farm and govern. Using China's "equal field" system as a model, the Japanese government took control of all private land and divided it equally among the peasants. Roads were built, and a tax system was set up.

The Taika Edict also raised Japan's ruler to the level of emperor, with divine authority and absolute power. To keep the old clan leaders happy, the emperor appointed them as governors and court officials.

The Nara Period

The emperor built a fabulous capital at Nara in 710. The city was carefully laid out on the model of the Chinese capital, Ch'ang-an. Religion, culture, and trade flourished in Nara. Traders brought precious goods from the faraway lands of China, India, and Persia. Nara's palaces and temples glittered with decorations of gold, silk, and exotic wood. Many of these riches can be seen today in the treasure house of Nara's Todai-ji Temple.

Nara's Todai-ji Temple

By order of the emperor, Japan's first histories were written—the *Kojiki* (*Record of Ancient Matters*) in 712 and the *Nihongi shoki* (*Chronicles of Japan*) in 720. These collections of oral traditions were part Shinto mythology and part real history. They described Japan's emperor as a divine figure, descended from the sun goddess.

Nevertheless, with the emperors' support, Buddhism spread throughout Japan. Buddhist temples acquired vast lands, and Buddhist priests were powerful court figures. The Daibutsu, an enormous bronze statue of Buddha, was erected in 752 in Nara, where it still stands today.

The Way of the Warrior

The samurai lived by a code of honor called *bushido* (the way of the warrior). Theirs was a life of virtue and dedication to duty, combining both Zen and Confucian ethics. Drinking alcohol, overeating, and gambling were prohibited. Armed with sword, spear, and bow and arrow, the samurai fought to keep order and protect their lords. They swore loyalty, even to the point of death.

The cherry blossom was the samurai's symbol. A samurai was willing to die in battle as petals fall from the flower. The samurai's sword was his badge of honor. If necessary to maintain his honor, the samurai took his own life *(seppuku)*.

control of the emperor's court. In the 1150s, rival bands of warriors fought for power until the Taira won out. Taira-no-Kiyomori became grand minister and put his family members in high court positions. In 1180, the emperor—overwhelmed and powerless—called to the provinces for help. Minamoto Yoritomo answered his master's call.

Yoritomo was one of the few leaders left from the defeated Minamoto clan. From his headquarters in Kamakura, he built up a huge following and vast holdings of land. In 1185, his armies beat the Taira and drove them out of Kyoto.

The Kamakura Period

The emperor rewarded Yoritomo with the power to appoint governors and tax collectors throughout Japan. In 1192, he was appointed *sei-i-tai shogun* (barbarian-conquering supreme general)—the court's highest military post. This made Minamoto Yoritomo the first of Japan's military governors. Shogunates, or military governments, ruled Japan from then until 1867—almost 700 years.

Yoritomo ran his *bakufu* (tent government) from Kamakura. It was a highly organized system. Various offices handled public policies, samurai affairs, job appointments, and legal problems. The *daimyo* (local warrior lords) swore loyalty to the shogun, and each daimyo had his own faithful army of samurai. Japan's feudal system was now firmly in place.

The samurai's biggest threat came from the Asian mainland. In the 1200s, fierce Mongol warriors were taking over much of Asia. Their leader, Kublai Khan, tried to conquer Japan, too. The samurai fought off one attack in 1274. Then, in 1281, as Mongol ships reached the Japanese coast, a violent typhoon smashed dozens of Mongol ships to bits on the shore. Ever after, the Japanese hailed this *kamikaze* (divine wind) that saved them from the Mongols.

Mongol leader Kublai Khan

The Muromachi Period

Fighting the Mongols had weakened the Kamakura government. In the 1330s, it was overcome by the Ashikaga clan. The Ashikaga general, Takauji, went on to fight the emperor's own army and put a new emperor on the throne. Takauji then had himself appointed supreme shogun, with his headquarters in the Muromachi district of Kyoto.

Japanese standards of beauty were set during this period. The Ashikaga shoguns built lavish temples and estates that still stand today. Among them are the Golden and Silver Pavilions in Kyoto. *No* dramas (plays that combine dance, acting, music, and poetry), landscape painting, and *chanoyu* (the tea ceremony) developed into high art forms.

Arts that were once reserved for the court now became widespread among the people. *Ikebana* (flower arranging) and gardening were especially popular. Buddhist communities designed gardens to reflect the harmony of nature.

As merchant ships traded with China, Japan's economy grew. Tradesmen organized guilds, and farmers grew crops for large-scale trade. Some villages became centers of production and manufacturing, while others became market towns.

Kinkakuji, the Temple of the Golden Pavilion of Kyoto

The Civil War Period

In time, the Ashikaga shoguns began losing their grip. Rival clans engaged in bitter power struggles. Beginning with the Onin War (1467–1477), Japan fell into more than one hundred years of civil war. Kyoto was burned to the ground, and the shoguns' power was broken at last.

Meanwhile, each daimyo had absolute authority over his domain. From his fortified castle, a daimyo tried to increase his landholdings, using his fighting force of samurai. Buddhist monasteries, too, acquired massive estates and protected them with armed forces.

In the midst of Japan's political chaos, European ships began to arrive. Portuguese, Dutch, British, and Spanish traders, as well as missionaries, landed on Japan's shores. In 1549, the Spanish priest Francis Xavier introduced Christianity to Japan.

Early seventeenth-century painting of Portuguese traders arriving in Nagasaki

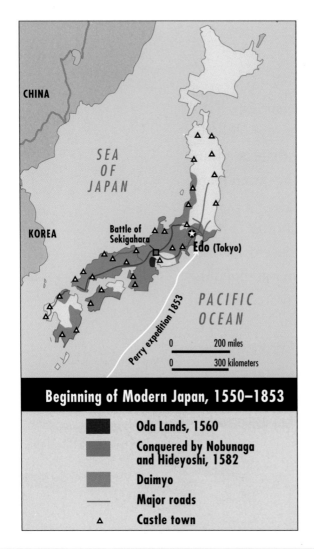

Beginning of Modern Japan, 1550–1853

- **Oda Lands, 1560**
- **Conquered by Nobunaga and Hideyoshi, 1582**
- **Daimyo**
- — **Major roads**
- △ **Castle town**

Map labels: CHINA, SEA OF JAPAN, KOREA, Battle of Sekigahara, Edo (Tokyo), Perry expedition 1853, PACIFIC OCEAN, 0 200 miles, 0 300 kilometers

The Three Unifiers

Three great warlords called the Three Unifiers helped to end the civil wars and usher in a new age. The First Unifier was Oda Nobunaga. Using newly developed firearms, he conquered many daimyo but was assassinated before he could finish his task.

Next came Toyotomi Hideyoshi. He succeeded in unifying Japan, but he died before reaching the rank of shogun. The Third Unifier was Tokugawa Ieyasu. Shortly after the Battle of Sekigahara in 1600, he was named supreme shogun of Japan.

Tokugawa Ieyasu

Tokugawa Ieyasu (1543–1616) was born into the Matsudaira clan. He called himself Tokugawa, the name of his ancestral village. Ieyasu crushed rival nobles in the Battle of Sekigahara (1600) and reunited Japan after a century of civil wars. The emperor declared him supreme shogun in 1603. Ieyasu established the Tokugawa shogunate, made Edo (present-day Tokyo) his capital, and built a great castle there. To keep his rivals in line, he required that all nobles live in Edo every second year. The life of Tokugawa Ieyasu is described in James Clavell's novel *Shogun.*

The Edo Period

Tokugawa Ieyasu moved the capital from Kyoto to Edo (present-day Tokyo). This began the Edo period, also called the Tokugawa shogunate. The Tokugawa reigned over a unified and powerful empire until 1867.

Society was now organized into clear levels. At the top were the samurai, led by the shogun and his immediate subordinates, the daimyo. Beneath them were farmers, craftspeople, merchants, and untouchables, or social outcasts. The *ronin* (masterless) were samurai who were independent—that is, unemployed. They were free, adventurous, romantic figures. Although they were masterless, they still belonged to the top class. Only the emperor was above all classes.

Many of the daimyo converted to Christianity. This worried the Tokugawa. They were afraid Christian foreigners wanted to take over Japan. In the 1620s, they began many bloody battles against Christians, executing thousands at a time.

During the 1630s, the Tokugawa drove all foreigners out of Japan and cut off foreign trade. Japan then remained closed to outsiders for more than 200 years. This

The Ninja

The *ninja* were special military forces. Spying, assassination, and sabotage were typical missions. Their skills and methods were tightly guarded family secrets. One ninja technique, or *ninjutsu*, was the art of making oneself invisible. Because the ninja did military "dirty work," people looked down on them. Nevertheless, their memory is honored at Ninja-dera Temple. Located on Sado Island near Niigata, it's a maze of narrow hallways and secret chambers.

The Forty-seven Ronin

Most Japanese people know the heroic story of the forty-seven samurai who avenged their lord's death. Every year in Edo, the Tokugawa shogun entertained important guests. He invited various lords to join in the festivities. During the 1701 party, Lord Asano struck Lord Kira with his sword. This was a grave offense. The shogun ordered Asano to commit suicide and seized his castle in Ako, west of Kobe. Asano's forty-seven samurai thus became ronin. However, they were sure that Kira had provoked their lord just to embarrass him, so they killed Kira to preserve Asano's honor. The shogun then had no choice but to demand the suicide of the ronin for the murder. The ronin quickly became popular heroes in Ako, with their own shrine and a gravesite with forty-seven wooden statues. Every year on December 14, the day of the murder, Ako honors the forty-seven ronin with a gala festival.

period of isolation was also a time of peace and culture. *Kabuki* and puppet theater, woodblock prints, and *haiku* poetry are among the art forms that developed.

Japan's doors were forced open in 1853 when Commodore Matthew Perry of the U.S. Navy sailed into Edo Bay with a fleet of "black ships"—warships spewing black smoke. Perry pressured the shogun into opening trade with the United States. British, Russian, Dutch, and French merchants soon followed.

The new "open door" policy was the undoing of the shogunate. Several daimyo in western Japan felt that the shogun was giving away too much to foreigners. In 1867, they raised an army and threw the shogun out.

A painting of Western traders in Yokohama

Artist Yoshitaki's woodblock print of Meiji leaders discussing the invasion of Korea in 1877

The Meiji Restoration

The emperor—powerless for centuries—was restored as the supreme ruler of Japan. The fifteen-year-old monarch lost no time exerting his power. He moved from Kyoto to Edo, named his reign *Meiji* (Enlightened Rule), and changed Edo's name to *Tokyo* (Eastern Capital). In 1889, the new Meiji Constitution went into effect. The following year, Shinto was made a state-supported institution and the guiding force in politics. As head of the nation, the emperor was exalted almost as a god-king.

Emperor Meiji abolished the feudal system, and with it, the traditional role of the samurai. All samurai had to turn in their swords, give up their fine lifestyles, and support themselves. The emperor's family and certain high-ranking samurai remained privileged classes, while all other Japanese became "commoners." Rebellious samurai took their last stand in the Satsuma Rebellion of 1877. In the shame of defeat, many committed suicide.

With no outside contact for so long, Japan had stood still in many ways. Other countries were making new discoveries in science and technology. Their farms and factories were using industrial machinery to produce more goods faster. Emperor Meiji quickly began to modernize. He set up a public school system, established an army and a navy, and built railroads. Western culture became the rage. Electricity, wheeled vehicles, and trolleys appeared on the streets of Tokyo.

Japan's ambitious industrial revolution was too expensive for the government to pay for by itself. Instead, it formed partnerships with private, family-owned companies called *zaibatsu*. The Mitsubishi zaibatsu was one of the first, and it grew to be one of the largest.

The Early Twentieth Century

With its new army, Japan fought wars with China (1894–1895) and Russia (1904–1905). After U.S. president Theodore Roosevelt negotiated a peace treaty in Portsmouth, New Hampshire, on September 5, 1905, Japan gained Korea, half of Sakhalin Island, and railroad rights in Manchuria.

In World War I (1914–1918), Japan joined the Allies in declaring war on Germany. Japan occupied the German-held Pacific Islands. Now a major military and industrial power, Japan joined the League of Nations in 1920.

Emperor Hirohito took the throne in 1926. He led Japan through some of the most critical events in its history. In 1931, Japan invaded China's northeast province of Manchuria, renaming it Manchukuo. In 1937, Japan occupied Shanghai and other large cities on China's east coast.

World War II

World War II broke out in Europe in 1939, and Japan became an ally of Germany and Italy. Meanwhile, tensions had been building between the United States and Japan for years. The U.S. government objected to Japan's aggressive moves in Asia. It responded by cutting off fuel and steel shipments to Japan and freezing Japanese assets in the United States. In the early morning of December 7, 1941, the Japanese bombed Pearl Harbor, a U.S. naval base in Hawaii. The United States immediately declared war.

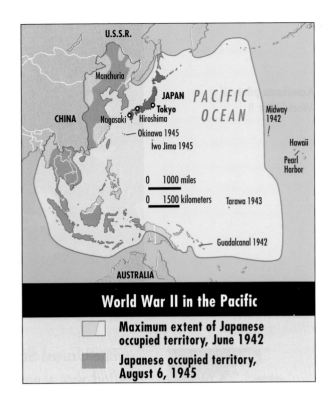

World War II in the Pacific

Maximum extent of Japanese occupied territory, June 1942

Japanese occupied territory, August 6, 1945

At first, things went well for Japan. By 1942, Japan occupied Southeast Asia, Indonesia, the Philippines and other Pacific islands, and some of Alaska's Aleutian Islands. Japanese suicide pilots crashed their planes into warships and other targets. They were named kamikaze pilots, after the "divine wind" that had saved Japan from the Mongols.

The Tides Turn

Japan's fortunes began to fall after its defeat in the Battle of Midway (June 1942). Costly losses followed at Guadalcanal and Saipan. At the Battle of Iwo Jima in February 1945, more than 20,000 Japanese soldiers were killed. Then the Allies began bombing Japan's coastal cities and industrial sites and cutting off its supply routes.

place in the international community. It joined the United Nations in 1956 and hosted the Olympic Games in 1964. Friendly relations were reopened with South Korea in 1965 and with China in 1972. The United States returned Okinawa to Japan in 1972, though it keeps its military bases there. At home, Japan began to address its pollution problems and social injustices.

Current Issues

In the 1980s, the United States and other countries began pressuring Japan to import more foreign products. They also complained that Japan's low-priced goods hurt their own home industries. Japan continues to work with its trading partners on these issues.

The 1990s were trying times for Japan. An earthquake devastated Kobe in 1995, and an extremist religious cult terrorized Tokyo with deadly gas on subway trains. Several prominent businessmen and government officials were involved in bribery scandals. In Okinawa, crimes by U.S. soldiers opened up old wounds over the U.S. military presence in Japan.

The Imperial Wedding

On June 9, 1993, thirty-two-year-old Crown Prince Naruhito married twenty-nine-year-old Masako Owada. The bride, a graduate of Harvard University, was a Japanese foreign-service officer before her marriage. Prince Naruhito, the oldest son of Emperor Akihito and Empress Michiko, is the future emperor of Japan. The centuries-old ceremony took place at Kashikodokoro (Place of Awe), a shrine on the grounds of Tokyo's Imperial Palace.

After decades of growth, the nation suffered an economic recession in the early 1990s. This led to a series of economic reforms. They aim to bring prices down and to make sure Japan remains a world leader in technology.

The imperial family still stands as a symbol of Japan's unity and dignity. Emperor Akihito's enthronement in 1989 and Crown Prince Naruhito's wedding in 1993 were ceremonial high points for the entire nation. Such events remind the Japanese people of their great good fortune. Through every catastrophe, present and past, their cherished traditions survive.

Crown Prince Naruhito and Princess Masako stand between Emperor Akihito and Empress Michiko.

Democracy in Action

The emperor is Japan's ceremonial head of state. According to the Meiji Constitution, the emperor traces his power back to the sun goddess. The 1947 constitution states that he draws his power from the will of the people. In any case, the Japanese people deeply respect the emperor as a symbol of their nation.

THE EMPEROR PRESIDES AT NATIONAL CEREMONIES AND presents honors and awards. He calls the Diet (the legislature) to order at the beginning of each session. However, the emperor has no governing powers. He must get the approval of the Diet for any important government acts.

Opposite: **The crowning of Emperor Akihito**

Japan's new constitution takes a firm stand for peace. It states that Japan forever rejects war as a way to settle international disputes. As part of this idea, Japan gave up its aggressive fighting forces. Today, Japan's army, navy, and air force are maintained only for self-defense.

The 1947 constitution gave women the right to vote for the first time in Japan's history. Today, every citizen who is at least twenty years old may vote. The constitution also guarantees freedom of expression.

Emperor Akihito

His Imperial Majesty Akihito, emperor of Japan, was born in 1933, the oldest son of Emperor Hirohito and Empress Nagako. He ascended to the throne upon his father's death in 1989, naming his reign *Heisei* (Peace and Concord). In 1959, he married Michiko Shoda, a commoner whom he met while playing tennis. In 1992, Akihito became the first Japanese emperor to visit China. He expressed regret for Japan's occupation of China from 1931 to 1945.

NATIONAL GOVERNMENT OF JAPAN

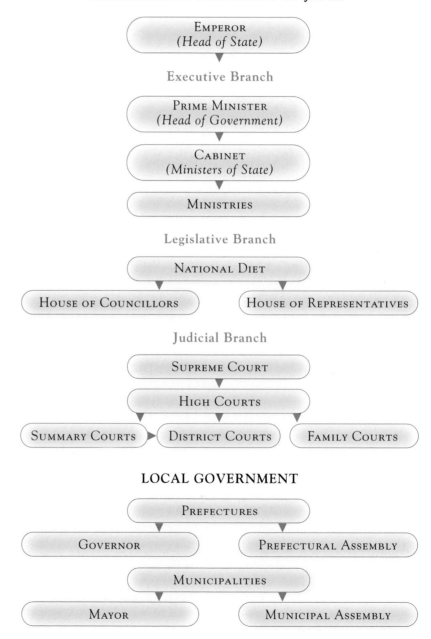

EMPEROR
(Head of State)

Executive Branch

PRIME MINISTER
(Head of Government)

CABINET
(Ministers of State)

MINISTRIES

Legislative Branch

NATIONAL DIET

HOUSE OF COUNCILLORS

HOUSE OF REPRESENTATIVES

Judicial Branch

SUPREME COURT

HIGH COURTS

SUMMARY COURTS

DISTRICT COURTS

FAMILY COURTS

LOCAL GOVERNMENT

PREFECTURES

GOVERNOR

PREFECTURAL ASSEMBLY

MUNICIPALITIES

MAYOR

MUNICIPAL ASSEMBLY

The Flag of Japan

Japan's national flag is white with a red disk in the center. Its Japanese name is *Hinomaru* (Circle of the Sun). The disk represents the sun, a 2,500-year-old symbol of the emperor as a descendant of the sun goddess. Japan adopted its flag in 1854.

The Legislature

Japan's lawmaking body is called the Diet. Like the U.S. Congress and the British Parliament, it is bicameral—composed of two houses. The upper house is the House of Councillors. Its 252 members are elected to six-year terms. Any citizen who is at least thirty years old may run for councillor. Every three years, half of the councillors' seats are up for election.

The Diet's lower house, the House of Representatives, is made up of 500 people. They serve four-year terms and must be at least twenty-five years old.

The Diet can carry on official business if at least one-third of the members are present. Ordinarily, it meets once a year, but emergency sessions may also be called.

The Diet is Japan's lawmaking body.

Kyoto's mayor leads a bicycle rally to appeal to citizens to protect the environment.

categories of city, town, and village. Cities are large urban areas. Villages are generally farming and fishing communities. In between are the towns. Each municipality elects a mayor and municipal assembly members to four-year terms.

When a municipality's population reaches about 1 million, it gets the powers of a prefecture in certain areas, such as city planning. In 1990, Japan had eleven municipalities in this category.

Ten Thousand Points of View

There are more than 10,000 registered political parties in Japan. Why so many? Japanese law requires any group that supports a candidate for public office to register as a political party. Most of these parties have followers in only a small region. Just a few parties are active in Japan's national politics.

It's sometimes said that Japan has a "one-and-a-half-party system." The Liberal Democratic Party (LDP) has been Japan's leading party since it was established in 1955. Until 1993, the prime minister and the majority of the Diet were LDP members.

The Japan Socialist Party (JSP) was Japan's second-ranking party for decades. In the mid-1990s, old parties began splitting to form new parties. One new force is Shinshinto, or the New Frontier Party (NFP). It was formed in 1994 when nine parties banded together. Its members want Japan to take a more forceful role in international relations.

Several other parties have strong followings, including Shinto-Sakigake, which split off from the LDP, and Minshuto, formed in 1996 by Social Democratic Party of Japan (SDPJ) and Shinto-Sakigake members. Komei (Clean Government Party) stands for human rights. It used to be the political arm of the Soka Gakkai sect of Buddhism, but they have now separated. The Japanese Communist Party has been gaining popularity in recent years.

Leaders of the Socialist Party celebrate a victory.

Ideas at War

In Japan, old and new political ideas are still at war. The great majority of the Japanese people are glad to have a democracy. Some, however, look back to pre–World War II times. They miss the days when Japan was an imperial power. They feel humiliated that outsiders forced so many changes on Japan.

Others believe that the constitution protects Japan's democracy. Without it, the people's human rights and political freedoms would be in danger. Conservatives in the Diet have tried to change the constitution and bring back some of the old ways. Their efforts have failed, however, as opposition parties resist them strongly.

The battle goes on in schools, too. Some of the older teachers remind their students of Japan's former days of glory. In contrast, many of Japan's schoolteachers feel a sense of guilt about Japan's past. In history classes, they stress the mistakes of the imperial government.

Japan's National Anthem

"Kimigayo"

("The Reign of Our Emperor")

Thousands of years
of happy reign be thine;
Rule on, my lord,
till what are pebbles now
By age united
to mighty rocks shall grow
Whose venerable sides
the moss doth line.

Tokyo

Tokyo, Japan's capital, began as the simple village of Edo. It became an important city when the Tokugawa shogun made it his capital in 1603. Then, when the Japanese emperor returned to power in 1868, he moved from Kyoto to Edo and renamed the city Tokyo, meaning "eastern capital."

Today, Tokyo is a world center of business and finance. The downtown area is a "concrete jungle" of towering skyscrapers, electronic billboards, and flashing neon signs. Sidewalks, subways, department stores, and boutiques are jammed with people.

Each area of Tokyo has its unique attractions. Shinjuku is the busiest commercial district, and Ginza is a famous shopping area. Roppongi offers discos, jazz clubs, and other nighttime entertainment. Akihabara is the place to buy electronics, and Tsukiji has the largest fish market in the world.

Dense crowds in Tokyo

Tokyo is also known for its beautiful gardens and parks. The Imperial Palace sits amid 250 acres (101 ha) in the heart of the city. In Yoyogi Park is the Meiji Shrine, one of Japan's most important Shinto shrines. Ueno Park, in northeastern Tokyo, is full of flowering trees, shaded walkways, temples, and shrines.

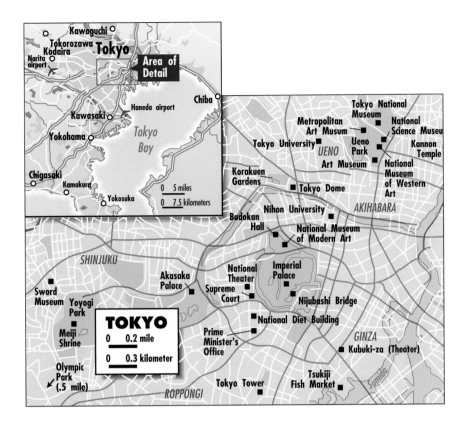

The city has more than 140 museums. Tokyo National Museum, the National Museum of Western Art, and the Metropolitan Art Museum stand in Ueno Park. Other museums highlight imperial treasures, paintings, woodblock prints, swords, and folk art.

Tokyo is also the best place to see the ancient arts of *kabuki* and *no* theater. *Sumo* wrestling matches are the most popular sports attraction.

Beyond the city itself are the ever-expanding suburbs. About 12 million people live in Tokyo's metropolitan area. Traveling between their homes and their jobs, commuters spend as much as three hours a day on trains.

Ingredients of an Economic Miracle

Japanese products are known all over the world today for their high quality. Japanese cars, electronic equipment, cameras, and watches are among the finest on the market. Names such as Sony, Toyota, and Kawasaki are well known, but many other companies—and some unique factors—contribute to Japan's success.

J APAN'S ECONOMY IS THE SECOND LARGEST IN THE WORLD. Only the United States has a higher gross national product (GNP). (The GNP is the total value of all the goods and services a country produces in a year.)

To get an idea of how productive Japan is, take a look at some figures. Its population is only about half the size of the U.S. population, but the average GNP per person in Japan is about $36,000. In the United States, the average GNP per person is only about $26,000.

Cost of Living

Japan's cost of living is the highest in the world. Here are some common items with their prices in 1997 U.S. dollars.

Item	Cost	Per
Ground beef	$20	2.2 lbs. (1 kg)
Bacon	$20–$40	2.2 lbs. (1 kg)
Bread	$6–$7.50	2.2 lbs. (1 kg)
Butter	$7	1.1 lb. (500 gm)
Milk	$1.75–$2.89	1.05 qt. (1 l)
Movie	$16.30–$27	ticket
Taxi	$250	one-way trip, airport to downtown Tokyo

Opposite: **The Shibuya district of Tokyo**

Cultural Currency

Japanese banknotes honor cultural values rather than political heroes. Philosopher and educator Yukichi Fukuzawa (1835–1901) appears on the ¥10,000 note. He studied Western education systems and founded Keio University. Pheasants appear on the reverse side. The ¥5,000 note shows educator Inazo Nitobe (1862–1933) on the front and Mount Fuji on the back. Novelist Soseki Natsume (1867–1916) and a pair of graceful cranes are on the ¥1,000 note. For the benefit of blind people, each banknote has raised marks that can be identified by touch.

Money Facts

The basic unit of currency in Japan is the yen (¥). Japanese coins come in values of ¥1 (one yen), ¥5, ¥10, ¥50, ¥100, and ¥500. Banknote values are ¥500, ¥1,000, ¥5,000, and ¥10,000.

Exchange rates between countries are constantly shifting. In mid-1998, ¥1 was equal to about 0.008 of one U.S. dollar, or four-fifths of one U.S. cent, and one U.S. dollar was equal to about ¥130. At the same time, ¥1 equaled about 0.005 of one Canadian dollar, or half of one Canadian cent, and one Canadian dollar was equal to about ¥90.

Manufacturing

Toyota, Honda, Nissan, Mitsubishi, Mazda—Westerners see these vehicles in their neighborhoods every day. Japan makes about 11 million cars, trucks, and buses a year—more than any other country in the world. Motor vehicles are Japan's top export, too, with the United States and Western Europe as its major customers.

Factory goods make up about 30 percent of Japan's GNP, and factories employ about 23 percent of all workers. Only the service industries use more people. About 60 percent of the labor force work for schools, hospitals, restaurants, banks, the government, and other service employers.

Japan also manufactures steel, ships, machinery, electrical and electronic equipment, and chemicals. Since the 1960s, the Japanese have been world leaders in electronic equipment. The cathode-ray tube, the transistor, and the computer chip were U.S. inventions. But it was the Japanese who turned them into useful con-

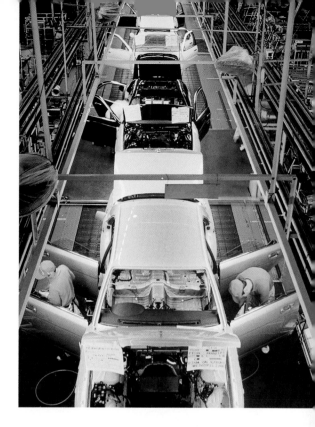

Car manufacturing is Japan's top industry.

What Japan Grows, Makes, and Mines	
Agriculture (1996)	
Rice	13,000,000 metric tons
Sugar beets	3,686,000 metric tons
Potatoes	3,400,000 metric tons
Manufacturing (1994)	
Semifinished steel	102,727,000 metric tons
Crude steel	98,686,000 metric tons
Cement	91,624,000 metric tons
Mining (1995)	
Limestone	201,089,000 metric tons
Silica stone	18,334,000 metric tons
Dolomite	3,773,000 metric tons

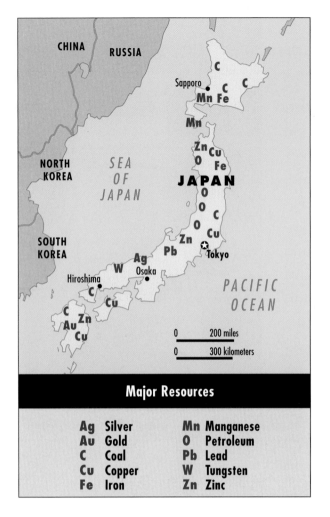

Major Resources

Ag	Silver	Mn	Manganese
Au	Gold	O	Petroleum
C	Coal	Pb	Lead
Cu	Copper	W	Tungsten
Fe	Iron	Zn	Zinc

On the island of Honshu, farmers harvest rice in terraced fields.

sumer products—TVs, radios, and personal computers.

Japan and the United States are major trading partners. About 30 percent of Japan's exports go to the United States, and about 23 percent of its imports come from the United States. After Canada, Japan is the biggest customer for U.S. goods.

Farms—So Much from So Little

In medieval times, Japanese farmers worked the land that belonged to their feudal lords. Often, it took more than half their crops to pay their taxes and rent. Only after World War II were most ordinary farmers able to buy their land. Most of Japan's farming still takes place on small, family-owned farms. The average farm covers fewer than 3 acres (1.2 ha).

Only about 15 percent of Japan's land can be farmed. Still, Japan produces about 60 percent of the food its people need. Japanese farmers make good use of the little land they have. They cut terraces, like steps, into hillsides and mountains. This provides more flat surfaces for growing crops.

Japan's Yayoi culture learned rice-cultivating methods from Korea in about 300 B.C. Today, rice takes up more than half of Japan's farmland. It grows in water-covered fields, or paddies, that are kept wet through irrigation. For hundreds of years, rice was planted and harvested by hand. Now, machines do almost all the work. In the warmer southern and western regions, rice farmers plant other crops after the rice is harvested.

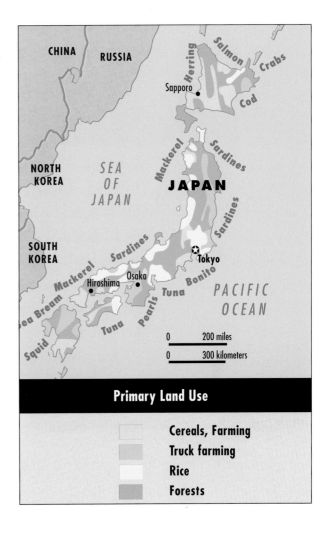

Primary Land Use

	Cereals, Farming
	Truck farming
	Rice
	Forests

In Hokkaido, farmers harvest giant white radishes called daikons.

Rice has become less important as new foods have come into the Japanese diet. In the 1930s, rice provided about 60 percent of a Japanese person's daily calories. Today, it provides less than 30 percent. Japan never imported rice until recently. In 1993, under pressure from international trading partners, Japan agreed to lift its ban on rice imports.

Other major crops are potatoes, cabbages, tea, sugarcane, sugar beets, and wheat. Strawberries, green peppers, and cucumbers are grown in greenhouses during the winter. This is possible in regions where the winters are sunny and city markets are nearby.

Japan's fruit trees yield apples, mandarin oranges, and pears. Other farm products include milk, beef, pork, chickens, and eggs. Hokkaido is known for its dairy farms, while many Kyushu farmers raise beef cattle.

Tea and Silk Traditions

Legend says that the Buddhist monk Saicho brought tea to Japan from China in A.D. 805. At first, the Japanese used it only as a medicine. Later it was used in Buddhist ceremonies and enjoyed by the elite at court. Today, Japanese green tea is known around the world. Many people believe that it promotes good health. Tokai is Japan's best tea-growing region.

Silk production, or sericulture, also has a long tradition in Japan. This delicate fiber is unwound from cocoons of the silkworm. Silk clothing once adorned emperors, court officials, and their ladies. Silk became an important export in the early 1900s, when Japan first became industrialized. Today, Japan is still an important silk producer. It exports silk thread, silk cloth, and silk clothing. However, the demand for silk has dropped since synthetic fibers arrived on the market.

Fishing

About half of the animal protein that the Japanese eat comes from fish and shellfish. Only in the last 100 years did the Japanese get used to red meat. Eating beef and pork was against traditional Buddhist beliefs.

Japan is one of the world's top fishing countries. Its fishing fleet is the largest in the world. Commercial fishing boats catch about 90 percent of Japan's seafood. The rest is raised on coastal "farms."

Fishers catch sardines, tuna, cod, herring, and salmon in the coastal waters. Japan hauls in more tuna than any other country in the world. Farm-raised seafood includes oysters, shrimp, octopus, and carp. The Japanese have also farmed seaweed for hundreds of years. It's an important part of their diet, either wrapped around *sushi* (vinegar-flavored rice) or eaten as a snack.

Diving for Abalone

Divers plunge into the waters of Suruga Bay to gather abalone. They use sharp knives to pry the soft seafood from the shell. Abalone is a delicacy, either cooked or raw. The shell's pearly lining is used in jewelry and for making decorative inlays in wood.

Fishers at Port Uwajima

The World's Largest Fish Market

Tsukiji, on Tokyo Bay, is the world's largest fish market. It sells more than 2,500 tons of fish a day.

In this bustling, early-morning street market, the business day ends around 8:00 A.M. About 17,000 trucks arrive in the wee hours, delivering fresh catches from Japan, Sri Lanka, and even the United States. Shoppers can choose from about 400 species of fish. For a snack, they can order from noodle and sushi shops.

The tuna auction begins at 5 A.M. and lasts for about an hour and a half. Auctioneers use hand and face gestures to make their deals. On average, they sell one tuna every four seconds!

Both private and commercial fishers once hunted whales. This changed when certain whale species became endangered. In the late 1980s, the International Whaling Commission imposed a worldwide ban on coastal whaling. This has been a hardship for people in northern coastal communities, who depended on whales for survival. Japan continues to appeal to the commission to allow these communities to hunt a limited number of the minke whale, a species that is not endangered.

Business—Family Style

Western executives study the Japanese style of business closely, looking for clues to its success. They find a jumble of remarkable features.

Japan's top companies used to hire an employee for life. Although this has changed, belonging to the company is like being part of a larger family. Workers see the good of the company as their highest goal. By helping the company, they help themselves. In Western tradition, it's often the reverse. Being an individual tends to be more appealing than joining the larger community.

A company picnic

Many family activities are connected to the company, such as picnics and other outings. The company often provides apartments for its workers, as well as loans and discounted goods. When business is slow, they still try to keep their employees. In short, companies take care of their employees, and in return, workers are fiercely loyal to their employers.

New employees are often hired right out of college or even high school. They're young and inexperienced, but they're trained on the job. Over time, they learn many skills and many facets of the business. Workers gradually rise in the ranks and get pay raises. As a rule, everyone moves up at about the same pace. No one zooms ahead of the others, and no one falls far behind.

Upper-level executives' salaries in Japan are the highest in the world (the United States ranks sixth). People usually retire at age fifty-five or sixty. A pension—income after retirement—begins at age sixty. It averages about 40 percent of the worker's salary.

Assembly-line workers exercise during their breaks.

The Workday Routine

In many large corporations, the workday begins with a physical exercise routine, followed by songs or cheers to create a positive attitude. The manager may give an encouraging talk or point out things that need special attention.

Employees are organized into small teams, or work groups. Each group is assigned tasks and problems. Team members share ideas and information to improve the company's performance. Anyone, regardless of rank, is welcome to make suggestions. The whole team shares the credit for good ideas. A failure or mistake is seen as a learning opportunity—a chance to make positive changes in how things are done.

Office workers put in about six weeks more per year than U.S. workers. They get more than a dozen holidays a year, but people rarely take their twenty days of vacation time. Working overtime and attending dinner meetings are considered normal parts of a job, and a workday can be eighteen hours long.

Some Downsides

Overwork is one drawback of the Japanese way of business. Work-related stress takes a toll on workers' health. The worst cases lead to *karoshi* (death by overwork). Today, people are demanding less pressure and shorter hours. Companies are responding with shorter workdays and "casual Fridays."

In the early 1970s, Japan's economy suffered a recession. For the first time ever, a major corporation laid workers off. This made people realize that their jobs were not as secure as they had imagined. Another recession struck in the early 1990s. More companies started using part-time and temporary workers, offering early retirement, and using foreign suppliers. Now, only about 30 percent of Japanese workers spend their entire career with one company.

Women make up about 40 percent of Japan's workforce. But they get less training, fewer promotions, and lower pay than men do, and few top executive positions are open to them. Japanese women are beginning to fight for equal rights. However, most companies have no policies to deal with sexual discrimination or harassment. And only about 15 percent of Japanese companies allow women to take time off to have a baby or care for their children. However, some companies are beginning to give both men and women time off to care for elderly parents.

Changes in the Work Ethic

Today, fewer young people are looking for lifetime jobs. Instead, they want jobs that are meaningful and enjoyable—jobs in which they can use their imagination. Unlike their parents, many don't believe that hard work is worth the trouble.

In a recent survey, college graduates were asked what they looked for in seeking a job. Four-fifths of them said that a five-day workweek was their top priority. They're no longer willing to work six or seven days a week with little or no vacation time. Instead, they place more value on social activities.

Quality control is very important in Japanese industry.

Women's Salaries

Working women in Japan make far less than men, compared with women in other industrialized countries.

Women's Salaries:

Country	Percentage of Men's Salaries
Australia	91
France	89
Germany	73
United States	69
Japan	60

A *geisha*, or female entertainer, waits for the bullet train.

Transportation

Japan's Shinkansen trains (bullet trains) are the fastest trains in the world. They run from Tokyo to Kyoto, Osaka, and other cities at speeds of more than 180 miles (290 km) an hour. All the big cities have underground metro trains, too. Both adults and children typically ride trains an hour or more each way to their offices and schools.

Trains help take the burden off Japan's roads and highways. Traffic jams are horrendous at rush hour and holiday time. In most cities, the street patterns are irregular. Cars, bicycles, and pedestrians are often crammed together in narrow side streets.

In the 1960s and 1970s, roadbuilding could barely keep up with the growing number of car owners. Now there are national and prefectural highways. Local roads reach rural areas, although many are not paved. Bridges connect the main islands. The Seikan Tunnel, under the Tsugaru Strait between Honshu and Hokkaido, is the world's longest undersea tunnel.

Japan Air Lines (JAL) and All Nippon Airways (ANA) are Japan's national airlines. Foreign flights use New Tokyo International Airport, usually called simply Narita Airport. It is located in the town of Narita, about 40 miles (64 km) outside Tokyo. Haneda, Tokyo's second airport, and dozens of other airports handle local flights within the country.

Japan has one of the largest fleets of merchant ships in the world. Ships dock at hundreds of ports along the coast. Tokyo-Chiba, Kobe, Osaka-Sakai, Nagoya, and Yokohama are the major international ports. About half of Japan's own local freight travels by water, too.

Communications

The Japanese are avid readers; they love the written word. More people buy daily newspapers in Japan than in any other country. Among more than 125 daily papers, the most widely read are *Yomiuri Shimbun*, *Asahi Shimbun*, and *Mainichi Shimbun*. The *Japan Times* is the most popular of the few English-language dailies. More than 2,700 monthly and 100 weekly magazines roll off Japan's high-tech presses, too. They cover news, sports, fashion, entertainment, cooking, and homemaking.

There is an average of one television set for every 1.2 people in Japan. That's almost twice as many TVs as there are telephones (one for every 2.1 people). All TV shows are in Japanese, although hotels receive English-language cable networks. Most radio broadcasts are in Japanese, but the Far East Network's programs are broadcast in English. Nippon Hoso Kyokai (NHK) is Japan's public TV and radio broadcasting corporation.

Living and Learning

Japan is home to about 126 million people—roughly half the size of the U.S. population. Yet the Japanese people are packed into an area smaller than the state of California. If that seems like a tight squeeze, consider this—about 90 percent of Japan's people live on 20 percent of the land. They are clustered in cities on the low-lying coastal plains.

In Japan, bridges connect one island with another.

Because mountains cover so much of Japan, the biggest cities lie in the lowlands along the coast. Tokyo, on Honshu Island's Tokyo Bay, is the capital and largest city. More than 8 million people live within the city limits. Tokyo's population density is about 37,000 people per square mile (14,286 per sq km). That's as tight as sixty-four people making their homes on a football field.

In contrast, suppose that all the Japanese people were spread evenly throughout the country. In that case, each person would have two-thirds of a football field for a living space.

Yokohama, Osaka, and Nagoya are Japan's next-largest cities after Tokyo. They, too, are on Honshu, facing the water. Eleven of Japan's cities have populations of more than 1 million people. Those on the southeast coast are the most populous.

Some cities are so close to one another that they flow together as a huge, combined urban area, or "conurbation." The Tokyo-Yokohama metropolitan area is the largest in the world, with more than 27 million people. Osaka-Kyoto-Kobe is another conurbation.

Opposite: **A fishing village in Washuzan**

Living and Learning **79**

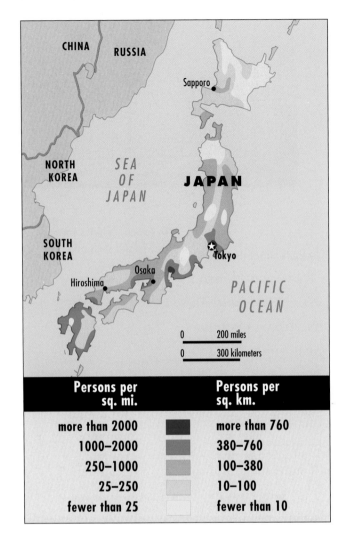

Persons per sq. mi.		Persons per sq. km.
more than 2000		more than 760
1000–2000		380–760
250–1000		100–380
25–250		10–100
fewer than 25		fewer than 10

Population of Japan's Largest Cities
(1990 census)

Tokyo	8,163,573
Yokohama	3,220,331
Osaka	2,623,801
Nagoya	2,154,793
Sapporo	1,671,742
Kobe	1,477,410
Kyoto	1,461,103

Who Are the Japanese People?

More than 95 percent of the people in Japan are ethnic Japanese. Among industrial countries, it's unusual for one ethnic group to be so widespread. From one point of view, a mixture of cultures increases diversity and makes a country stronger. But for the Japanese, their common heritage is their strength. It has enabled them to move forward with shared values and a sense of unity.

Japan's small ethnic minority groups include Korean, Chinese, and Ainu people. About 700,000 Koreans and 70,000 Chinese people live in Japan.

The Ainu

The Ainu are a tribal people who live mainly on Hokkaido Island. Ainu also live on the Kuril and Sakhalin islands to the north. Ancestors of the Ainu lived in Japan before Asian people migrated there. Gradually, they were driven farther north. Today, there are only about 15,000 to 20,000 Ainu left.

Ainu people are usually classified as Caucasian, while the Japanese, Koreans, and Chinese are Mongoloid. The Ainu have light skin, round eyes, and wavy hair. Ainu men are known for their full beards.

Traditionally, the Ainu lived in villages of thatched-roof houses. They survived by hunting, fishing, and farming. In their religious beliefs, they recognized a spiritual power in the mountains, winds, and other natural things. Fire was given special reverence, and the bear was seen as a sacred animal. Today, most Ainu live as other Japanese people do. But they are still discriminated against in many ways.

As a tiny ethnic minority, the Ainu miss out on schooling and social benefits available to other Japanese. Like Native Americans, they have seen their land and their rights disappear over the years. The Ainu have formed a civil rights group to fight for better treatment.

An Ainu woman demonstrates weaving cloth on a hand loom at a village museum.

The Burakumin

The *burakumin* are not an ethnic minority but a social minority. Their ancestors in the Edo period were an outcast class. Burakumin held jobs that were considered "unclean," such as butcher or leatherworker. Today, the burakumin—making up about 3 percent of the population—are still a lower social class. They live in poor neighborhoods or in towns of their own.

The constitution forbids discrimination, but the burakumin are almost locked into their position. They have a hard time getting into good jobs, apartments, and schools. Marriages between burakumin and non-burakumin are considered scandalous. Recently, the burakumin have organized a political association that works to improve their status.

Japanese Language and Writing

Practically everyone in Japan speaks Japanese, the official language. Different dialects are spoken in various regions, but Tokyo's dialect, the standard form, is used in schools, radio and TV, business, and government.

When speaking, a Japanese person may use several "levels" of speech. Each level uses different forms of verbs, adjectives, and nouns. The level shows the speaker's attitude toward the subject or the person being addressed. For example, a boy would speak to his teacher one way and to his sister another way.

Signs fill the streets of Toyko.

Forms of Japanese Writing

The Japanese write with three different types of script. *Kanji* consists of Chinese characters, or picture-symbols. Each character stands for a word or an idea.

Before World War II, an educated Japanese person had to know thousands of kanji characters. In 1946, the government listed 1,850 characters for common use, and more were added in 1981, for a total of 1,945 characters. Students in elementary school must learn 881 of those.

The other two Japanese scripts are phonetic, with symbols that stand for sounds. *Hiragana* characters are used to write Japanese words that do not occur in Chinese. Ninth-century court ladies devised hiragana to write poems and stories.

Katakana is used for words that are borrowed from Western languages. Japanese written in the Roman (Western) alphabet is called *romanji*. All the Japanese words in this book are written in romanji.

Japanese writing goes from top to bottom, instead of left to right. A written page begins in the upper right-hand corner. Each line is written to the left of the previous line. Japanese books begin at what Westerners would call the "back" and read through to the "front." Newspapers, however, use both top-to-bottom and left-to-right styles.

Names

The Japanese place the family name first and the given name last. The film director known in the West as Akira Kurosawa is Kurosawa Akira in Japan. (By law, a person may have only one given name.) The ending *-san* is often added to a name as a gesture of respect. For instance, a neighbor whose family name is Tanaka would be called Tanaka-san. Teachers are addressed with *-sensei* added to their names.

Common Japanese Expressions

yes	**hai** (HAH-ee)
no	**iie** (ee-EH)
thank you	**domo arigato** (DOH-moh ah-REE-gah-toh)
excuse me	**sumimasen** (soo-MEE-mah-sehn)
good morning	**ohayo gozaimasu** (oh-HAH-yoh goh-ZAH-ee-mahs)
good day	**konnichi wa** (KOHN-nee-chee-wah)
good night	**oyasumi nasai** (oh-YAH-soo-mee nah-sah-ee)
good-bye	**sayonara** (sah-YOH-nah-rah)

Japanese Language Pronunciation

The Japanese language has five vowel sounds: **a**, **e**, **i**, **o**, and **u**. Each syllable in a word gets fairly equal stress.

a	*a* as in f*a*ther
e	*e* as in m*e*t
i	in the middle of a word, *i* as in p*i*n at the end of a word, *ee* as in fr*ee*
o	*o* as in s*o*
u	*oo* as in n*oo*n
g	hard *g*, as in *g*o at the end of a word, *ng* as in ri*ng*
w	*wh* as in *wh*ich

Other consonants are pronounced as they are in English. An exception is *r*, whose sound is a cross between *r* and *l*.

The Education System

In Japan's feudal period, nobles and samurai set up schools for their own children. Public education began in 1872. Today, Japanese children are required to attend school from ages six through fifteen. However, many start their education earlier than age six. Parents want their children to have a good future, and that means doing well in school from the very beginning.

The kindergarten system provides education for ages three through six. Elementary school begins at six and lasts for six years. Lower secondary school (middle school) lasts for three years. By that time, students have fulfilled their school obligations.

However, about 97 percent of fifteen- to eighteen-year-olds go on to upper secondary school. Students who are aiming for college take courses in many subject areas. Those on a vocational track might study agriculture, fine arts, or technical subjects.

Juku—private "cram schools"—exist from nursery school through the higher levels. They offer two to three hours of after-school instruction, two or three days a week. They help students prepare for the entrance exams to top-notch high schools and colleges.

Junior high school students studying

Almost half the nation's high-school graduates go on to college. Japan has more than 500 universities that offer both four-year degrees and graduate-school programs. Nihon University in Tokyo, with about 80,000 students, is the largest university, but Tokyo University (*Todai*) is the most prestigious. Its graduates can expect to get the best jobs in government and industry. Kyoto University is another high-ranking school. In addition, thousands of Japanese students attend colleges overseas.

Junior colleges have two-year programs. Most technical colleges offer five years of specialized training, while other technical schools compress their training into a shorter time span.

Numbers, One to Ten

Ichinisan is the Japanese word for counting by number. It's made of the words for one, two, and three. The numbers one through ten in Japanese are:

1	ichi	6	roku
2	ni	7	shichi
3	san	8	hachi
4	shi	9	ku
5	go	10	ju

A Day at School

Japanese students attend classes 5$\frac{1}{2}$ days a week. Saturday is a half-day, with one or two Saturdays off every month. The school year begins in April. Summer vacation lasts from late July to the end of August. Winter vacation (December–January) and spring vacation (March) last about ten days each.

Students carry their books and lunch in a backpack. In most schools, uniforms are required. Unusual hairstyles and behavior are frowned upon, even by fellow students. During recess, schoolchildren climb on playground equipment, play soccer, or jump rope. Mothers send their children off to school with a *bento* box—a boxed lunch with the courses laid out in an artistic way. Some schools provide a classroom lunch.

In elementary school, children study arithmetic, science, social studies, literature, music, crafts, and physical education. For boys, physical education might include martial arts and for girls, gymnastics or dance. There are also classes in calligraphy. National-language class includes haiku (poetry) writing, and art includes origami (paper folding). Middle school continues with the same subjects, adding English.

Students clean their own schools. On field days, they have sports contests, visit museums and cultural shows, or take trips to other cities. Most students belong to an after-school sports, science, or music club.

As part of their public-service program, students ask for blood donations.

Competition, Pressure, and Shame

Competition in Japanese schools is tough and begins as early as kindergarten. At each level of education, students take exams to qualify for the next higher level. At the top is the all-important college-entrance exam. Getting into a prominent university guarantees a good job with a high-ranking company or government agency.

Japanese students are under tremendous pressure. For many children, their exams are the most important thing in their lives. Many families hire private tutors to help their children prepare for exams. Some students also attend "cram schools" in addition to regular classes. Naturally, not everyone passes.

High school track-and-field competition teaches teamwork. By running with their feet tied together, students learn the importance of cooperation.

Failing an exam is considered a matter of personal shame and a disgrace to the family. The effects of this pressure can be tragic. Japan suffers a high rate of suicide among its young people, and failing exams is the major reason. Competition also leads to bullying and violence among students. Some children suffer so badly from such pressures that they refuse to go to school.

The Battle of the School Systems

In Japan, nearly 100 percent of adults can read and write, while in the United States, the literacy rate is only 79 percent. This raises many arguments about which country's school system is better.

In Japan, education relies heavily on memorizing facts. Individuality and creative thinking are considered significant only after a student has a solid foundation of knowledge and skills. Also, nationwide standards outline what a student should know at each level.

In contrast, the United States has a more relaxed educational system. Different school districts have different standards for what students should know, what they wear, and how they behave. Many schools put a high value on creativity and individuality.

Job Skills

U.S. employers often complain that job applicants lack basic skills—reading, writing, and arithmetic. Younger employees, they say, don't work hard or try to rise to a higher level.

Nobel Prize Winners from Japan

Name	Year	Field
Hideki Yukawa	1949	Physics
Sin-itiro Tomonaga	1965	Physics
Yasunari Kawabata	1968	Literature
Leo Esaki	1973	Physics
Eisaku Sato	1974	Peace
Kenichi Fukui	1981	Chemistry
Susumu Tonegawa	1987	Physiology or Medicine
Kenzaburo Oe	1994	Literature

On the other hand, Japanese-educated people often have more to offer when they apply for technical jobs. They have good math skills, know the metric system, and can think clearly and logically. They also have a strong desire to achieve more.

Some critics say that the Japanese system keeps students from coming up with new ideas. Japanese business managers recognize this, too—especially in companies that have to keep inventing new products to stay in business. Still, Japanese schools are good at providing the whole population with the basic skills they need to succeed as adults.

More Japanese women are being trained for highly skilled jobs.

Ways of the Spirit

Shinto is the native religion of Japan. Traces of Shinto beliefs and practices have been found from as early as A.D. 300. The Meiji government made Shinto a state institution. Today, the constitution separates religion from politics, guaranteeing equal religious freedom to everyone.

Religions of Japan

Shinto and related religions	51.3%
Buddhism	38.3%
Christianity	1.2%
Other	9.2%

J APAN'S ANCIENT RELIGION IS *SHINTO,* MEANING "THE WAY OF the *kami*" or "the way of the gods." Shinto beliefs and practices are deeply rooted in Japanese culture. Most Japanese who follow Buddhism or Christianity also practice Shinto customs. In fact, it is not unusual for a person to have a Shinto wedding and a Buddhist funeral.

Opposite: **Chion-In Temple in Kyoto**

The Japanese honor their ancestors at local Shinto shrines.

The Kami

At the heart of Shinto are the *kami,* or divine spirits. The kami are believed to oversee human life and the ways of the world, bringing either good fortune or chaos.

Some kami are the spirits of ancestors. In Shinto's earliest days, each clan honored its ancestral kami. Other kami are the spiritual forces in nature and the environment. They govern the weather and seasons, residing in rain, fire, mountains, animals, or trees.

Izanagi and Izanami are the spirit parents of the Japanese islands. Izanagi's daughter, Amaterasu, is Shinto's highest deity. She is

Buddhism Comes to Japan

Fragments of Buddhist teachings were known in Japan as early as the fifth century. About 538, a Korean king sent a statue of Buddha and some Buddhist scriptures to the Japanese court. Prince Shotoku embraced the teachings. He made Buddhism Japan's official religion, included Buddhist teachings in his constitution, and built many monasteries and temples.

Statues outside the Buddhist Zenko-ji Temple in Nagano

At first, Buddhism was reserved mainly for the emperor's court. In the un-rest of the Kamakura period (1192–1338), new sects arose that offered hope. Then the faith spread to warriors and common people. Buddhism did not replace Shinto in the people's minds and hearts, though. Beloved Shinto gods came to be seen as alternate identities of Buddhist deities.

Buddhist Sects Today

Many Buddhist sects, or schools of thought, came to Japan from India via China and Korea. Some sects died out, while others flourished. In time, Japanese Buddhism took on its own unique form.

Siddhārtha Gautama: The Buddha

Siddhārtha Gautama was a wealthy Indian prince born about 563 B.C. He gave up his rich lifestyle to ponder why there was so much suffering in this world. In utter poverty and simplicity, he meditated for five years until he understood. From that moment, he became known as the *Buddha*, meaning "Enlightened One."

The Buddha determined that all suffering is the result of desire, hatred, and ignorance. By removing these, a person can break free from pain and reach enlightenment.

This enlightened state is called *nirvana*. Reaching that point may take many reincarnations, or rebirths in another life. In Japanese Buddhism, the similar term *satori* is the sudden awakening to one's own Buddha nature.

Buddhism spread through India and Sri Lanka and into Tibet, China, and Korea. The Mahayana version of Buddhism is the one that took root in Japan. One of its central ideas is the *bodhisattva*—an enlightened being who is devoted to helping others on their path.

More than 100 Buddhist sects exist in Japan today. Some are very old, surviving from the Nara period. The Tendai, Shingon, Zen, Pure Land, and Nichiren sects became the most widespread. They are Japan's major Buddhist sects today.

Buddhist monks perform a ceremony in honor of Buddha's birthday.

Tendai and Shingon Sects

Two Buddhist monks spread Tendai and Shingon teachings in early 800. About one-third of Japan's Buddhists belong to the Tendai sect. Founded by the monk Saicho, Tendai is based on teachings in the *Lotus Sutra*, a scripture on the Buddha's life. Believers see the Buddha's nature within every person. Thus, everyone has the ability to become an enlightened being.

The monk Kukai taught Shingon beliefs in Japan. This sect sees the universe as a reflection of Buddha's nature. With our human vision, we can see only small parts of this reality. Shingon has many mystical secrets and magical aspects.

Ways of the Spirit **95**

Saicho

Saicho (A.D. 767–822), also known as Dengyo Daishi, founded Japan's Tendai sect of Buddhism. Saicho lived alone for many years on Mount Hiei, near Kyoto, and built a monastery there. After studying Buddhism in China, he decided that Tendai was the best form. He returned to Japan, where he taught many followers. Three thousand temples were built around his monastery.

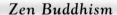

Zen Buddhism

Zen is the best-known form of Buddhism in the West. However, only about 10 percent of Japanese Buddhists follow it. The Indian master Bodhidharma (Daruma in Japanese) brought Zen teachings to China. From there, Zen came to Japan in the twelfth century.

The word *Zen* means "meditation." According to Zen, a person becomes enlightened by meditating—not by studying scripture or performing rituals. Zen finds beauty in ordinary things. In the Zen point of view, any act of everyday life can be a form of meditation that brings enlightenment.

Zen's simplicity appealed to the common people. Simple home activities, such as arranging flowers or serving tea, became meaningful spiritual arts. Zen was also popular with the samurai. It gave them a way to lift their fighting arts to a higher level. Zen appealed to artists, too. It sharpened their view of the beauty in the natural world.

Kukai

Kukai (A.D. 774–835), also known as Kobo Daishi, spread Shingon Buddhist teachings in Japan. Kukai studied with Chinese and Indian Buddhist masters. He founded a monastery, and Kongobuji Temple on Mount Koya near Osaka became the center of his teachings. Some say that Kukai never died but entered a state of deep meditation to await the reappearance of the Buddha. Even today, a monk regularly changes the robes on Kukai's remains.

Learning the Ways of Zen

Zen itself broke into two sects. In 1191, the monk Eisai founded the Rinzai sect, which favors instant enlightenment. A Rinzai master uses the *koan* to teach Zen principles to his students. The typical koan is a question with no answer. It could be a riddle or a story that seems to make no sense. Puzzling over the koan leads the student to a flash of understanding. A famous koan is "What is the sound of one hand clapping?"

Dogen, a student of Eisai, founded the Soto sect of Zen. Its followers practice *zazen*, or sitting meditation. Under the personal guidance of a master, the student studies meditation, the sutras, and the life of the Buddha. Enlightenment comes not just by meditating, but by doing everyday activities in a thoughtful way.

Pure Land Buddhism

The Pure Land (*Jodo*) sects are the most widely followed forms of Buddhism in Japan today. Believers hope to be reborn into the paradise of the Western Kingdom, or Pure Land. This is the realm of the compassionate Buddha Amitabha (called Amida in Japan), the Buddha of Immeasurable Light.

Pure Land Buddhism arose in the twelfth century, around the same time as Zen. Honen, a Tendai monk, taught that a person needs only faith and prayer to reach enlightenment. In the sutras he found the mantra, or prayer, "*Namu Amida butsu*" ("Hail to the Buddha Amida"). Followers recite this mantra with complete faith in the power of Buddha Amitabha's love.

Daruma

Daruma is a popular figure in Japanese tradition. It's said that he sat meditating until his legs fell off. Daruma figures—with no legs—are said to bring good luck or protect the owner. The Daruma figures given as New Year's gifts have no eyes. When you have a wish or a goal, you paint in one of the eyes. When you reach your goal, you then paint in the other eye.

Flower arranging is a Zen tradition.

Honen's student Shinran made enlightenment even simpler. He founded the True Pure Land (*Jodo Shin*) sect. According to Shinran, the Buddha did not want people to follow complicated practices. Instead, he said, a person needs only faith to reach the Pure Land. For Shinran, "Even a thief can be saved."

Shinran made Buddhism easier to practice. He removed rules against eating meat, abolished rigorous discipline, and allowed Buddhist priests and monks to marry. Jodo Shin became popular in Japan's feudal society. Because it reaches out to everyone equally, the sect is popular today, too.

Soka Gakkai

Sects called the New Religions were popular after World War II. Most widespread is Soka Gakkai, a branch of Nichiren Buddhism. In the thirteenth century, the monk Nichiren gained a wide following. He preached that Buddhism could flourish only in a peaceful country that observed the teachings of the Buddha.

Soka Gakkai claims several million believers in Japan and in other countries as well. Members focus on world peace and cooperation, based on Buddhist principles.

Christianity

In 1549, the first Christian missionary arrived in Japan. He was Francis Xavier, a Jesuit priest. Other missionaries sailed in on Portuguese and Dutch trading ships. Christianity flourished for a short time until it was banned in 1587. Under the Tokugawa shogunate, Christians were severely persecuted.

A Christian wedding in a Tokyo cathedral

Since 1873, Christians have been free to practice their religion in Japan. Christianity was accepted even more after World War II, as Western ideas flooded in. Today, less than 2 percent of the Japanese people are Christians. Most are Catholic, but there are Anglican and United Church of Christ members as well. Christians operate many schools, hospitals, and social agencies throughout the country.

Confucianism

Hardly anyone speaks of Japan as a Confucian country. But Confucian values are like the air: They are everywhere in Japanese life.

Confucianism is based on the teachings of the Chinese philosopher Confucius (551–479 B.C.). He taught rules for orderly living, rather than a formal religion. Confucian ideas came to Japan in the fifth century. They fit in well with the Shinto idea of a divine emperor. Japan's Prince Shotoku reorganized his own government to reflect Confucian principles.

Loyalty and respect are the highest virtues in Confucianism. Their value is evident in Japanese speech and society. Family loyalty spreads out to the larger "families" of the company and the nation. Respect is given to parents and ancestors as well as to employers and the emperor.

A Confucian shrine in Nagasaki

Ancient Traditions in a Modern World

In its early days, Japan imported arts from China and Korea. Mixed with local culture, these arts became uniquely Japanese. Sports, too, combine native culture and imports. They range from Shinto-inspired sumo wrestling and samurai-based martial arts to Western baseball.

Flowers, Trees, and Gardens

*I*KEBANA, THE ART OF FLOWER ARRANGING, IS MORE THAN 1,400 years old. When Buddhism first came to Japan, people offered flowers at shrines of the Buddha. Later, ikebana became a nonreligious art, practiced at court and in private homes. In this art, not only the flowers, but also the vase, leaves, and branches are important. They are all arranged to express harmony among Heaven, Earth, and humans.

Bonsai is the art of growing dwarf trees. Growers carefully trim the branches and roots to stunt the tree's growth. On its tiny landscape, the tree seems to blend perfectly with its natural habitat. Some bonsai look like ancient, windswept pines on a rocky mountainside. Families might pass down a treasured bonsai from generation to generation for hundreds of years.

A bonsai artist admires his work.

Gardens adorn Japanese homes, temples, and public places. Zen monks once designed gardens to aid meditation. They arranged stones, water, and plants in harmonious and thought-provoking ways. In dry landscape gardens, sand, stones, and shrubs are arranged to look like mountains and water. In Zen

Opposite: **Osaka Castle and Twin Towers**

Ancient Traditions in a Modern World   **101**

A Zen rock garden

rock gardens, white pebbles are raked in wavy patterns to mimic the sea. The tea gardens outside tea houses prepare a person for the tea ceremony.

The Way of Tea

Chanoyu, the tea ceremony, was once reserved for the highest classes. Nobles and samurai built a separate tea house, specially designed for peace of mind. The elaborate tea ritual has rules for every detail—the way of moving, the room, its decorations, and even the garden outside.

Flowers or a hanging scroll often decorate the tea room. The tea must be powdered green tea—preferably the tea grown in Uji, near Kyoto. Utensils include a bamboo whisk, a tea scoop, a lacquered tea bowl, and a tea container.

The host carries the utensils into the room, placing each object in a precise position. Both host and guest sit on the floor—kneeling, then sitting back on the heels—while water

Master of the Way of Tea

The tea master Sen Rikyu (1521–1591) was born into a wealthy merchant family in Sakai. An ardent student of Zen, he refined the Way of Tea, based on four principles: harmony, respect, purity, and tranquillity. Rikyu served as Master of the Tea Ceremony to both Oda Nobunaga and Toyotomi Hideyoshi. For unknown reasons, Hideyoshi commanded Rikyu to commit suicide. Rikyu's descendants founded various schools of tea service.

boils over a charcoal fire. The host pours water into the teacup and whips it with the whisk until it foams. Tiny, sweet tea cakes are served with the tea.

Architecture

The oldest buildings in Japan today are temples and shrines. Horyuji Temple, built in Nara in 607, is Japan's oldest place of worship. In later centuries, nobles and samurai built homes with a steep, cypress-bark–thatched roof, wooden pillars and floors, and folding screens. Kyoto's Imperial Palace was built in this style. With the tea ceremony came the tea-house style, usually including beautifully landscaped gardens. Even castles were built with beauty in mind.

After the Meiji Restoration in 1868, Western-style brick and stone became common in offices, factories, and government buildings. However, they failed to stand up to the 1923 Tokyo earthquake. Steel-and-concrete construction turned out to be the most earthquake-proof.

Japanese Castles

Huge stone castles from medieval times are found throughout the Japanese countryside. Matsumoto, Nagoya, Osaka, Kyoto, and Tokyo are just a few of Japan's castle towns. Himeji-jo Castle (above) near Kobe is one of the most beautiful. Called the White Crane, it was first built in the fourteenth century and expanded by Toyotomi Hideyoshi in 1581. Typical castles are several stories high, with slanted roofs on each level. Many have towers, triangular gables, and slits in the walls for shooting arrows or guns.

Today, high-rise apartment and office buildings solve the problem of a large population on a limited land area. Architects are also finding ways to mix historic and modern elements. One example is Tokyo's Yoyogi National Stadium, designed by architect Kenzo Tange for the 1964 Olympics.

Music, New and Old

Every year, hundreds of teenagers try out to be the next *idoru kashu*, or singing idol. Talent agencies sponsor the contests, train the chosen few to sing and dance, and promote their careers. Most idoru are quickly forgotten, but some become stars. They appear on TV shows, and magazines publish every detail of their lives for adoring fans.

This is a far cry from the music scene in Japan's early days. The emperor's orchestra played court music called *gagaku*. Each instrument played a mythical role. The *sho*, a standing instrument made of seventeen bamboo tubes, shed light from the heavens. The oboelike *hichiriki* spoke the voices of Earth,

Traditional Music and Instruments

Traditional Japanese music uses a pentatonic, or five-note scale; ornamental notes; and vibrato, the wavering or vibrating of one note. The instruments that produce these sounds developed over many centuries. The *koto* is a zitherlike instrument with thirteen strings. It lies flat, either on the ground or on a table. The *samisen* is like a banjo, with a long fingerboard and three strings. Another string instrument, the *biwa*, is pear-shaped, with four or five strings. The *shakuhachi* is a long bamboo flute. *Taiko* (drums) come in all sizes and sounds, from small, high-pitched models to huge, thunderous drums.

and the *ryuteki* (a flute) was a dragon dancing in the sky. Gagaku is still around today, though it is rarely performed.

All Japan's major cities have concert halls. They showcase everything from Western classical music to jazz, rock, and the idoru kashu of the day. Tokyo alone has nine full-time orchestras. Hundreds of city and university orchestras throughout the country play Japanese and Western classical music.

Some Japanese musicians are also famous in the Western music world. Seiji Ozawa conducts both the Boston Symphony Orchestra and the New Japan Philharmonic Orchestra. Sopranos Atsuko Azuma and Yasuko Hayashi are international opera stars. Many young Japanese pianists and violinists win top prizes in international competitions.

Dramatic Arts

No plays were once the official dramas of the upper class. These serious plays combine dance, acting, music, and poetry. The main character begins as an ordinary man or woman, then reveals his or her true identity as a legendary person or supernatural being. A traveling priest is another essential character. In the background, a chorus fills in the details of the story. In the past, the masked performers were men, but women play some parts now. Short comedies called *kyogen* are performed between the acts of a no play.

Kabuki plays, on the other hand, grew up among the common people. They feature elaborate costumes and makeup and an exaggerated acting style. The plots are historical tales or scenes from everyday life.

Kabuki performers

Kabuki began with the maiden Okuni, who performed in the dry riverbeds of Kyoto in the seventeenth century. The shows became popular with the townspeople and grew into an elaborate form. Traditionally, all kabuki players were men.

Bunraku is Japan's traditional puppet theater. The puppets are large and moved not with strings but by hand. Sometimes two or three people operate the different body parts of each puppet.

Arts of the Brush

Calligraphy (*shodo*) is the art of painting Japanese writing symbols. Calligraphers use a brush and black ink to make strong, graceful strokes. They have only one chance to "do it right." Once the ink contacts the paper, it can't be changed.

Japanese screen prints are paintings on folding panels of paper or silk. They may depict rambling landscapes of hills and villages, historic journeys, or famous battles. Ink painting began as early as A.D. 700. The artists used black ink, creating dramatic effects with shades of gray.

Woodblock prints (*ukiyo-e*) became popular in the Edo period. It takes several artists to make one print. One paints the basic picture, and another carves a separate woodblock for each color. Other artists make the paper, mix the inks, paint the inks onto the woodblocks, and print the colors onto the

Tokyo National Museum

Tokyo National Museum, in Ueno Park, is the largest museum in Japan. Before 1868, the site was the principal Buddhist temple of the Edo period. The museum displays fine arts and archaeological objects, and many are designated as national treasures or important cultural properties. There is a fine collection of samurai swords, as well as Chinese, Korean, and Indian artifacts.

Sesshu and the Mouse

Sesshu (1420–1506) was one of Japan's greatest black-ink artists. According to legend, Sesshu grew up in a temple, where he studied to become a monk. He was more interested in painting, however, and neglected his studies. As a punishment, his teacher tied him to a pillar. Sesshu wept and his tears made a puddle on the floor. Using his toes, he painted the figure of a mouse in the puddle. His teacher was so moved by the lifelike mouse that he allowed Sesshu to continue painting.

paper one by one. Popular subjects include an aspect of nature or a beautiful woman. Katsushika Hokusai's *Thirty-Six Views of Mount Fuji* is a famous series of woodblock prints.

Japanese woodwork is a fine art.

Traditional Crafts

Japanese woodwork is known for its fine craftsmanship. One prized item is the lacquered wooden chest with iron-plate fittings. Furniture makers in the Matsumoto area have practiced their craft since the sixteenth century. They make almost unbreakable furniture whose joints fit together without nails.

Ancient Traditions in a Modern World

Japanese dishware is made in a variety of materials. Round tubs for rice, seafood, and wine are made from cypress wood. Ceramic vases and jars are made by baking clay at high temperatures and coating it with a shiny glaze. Lacquerware dishes and boxes are painted with several coats of varnish for a hard, mirrorlike finish. Some are inlaid with shell, painted with gold leaf, or sprinkled with gold dust.

Metalwork is another traditional Japanese art. Master sword makers have passed down their skills for more than 1,000 years. During the Kamakura period, sword-making became a fine art. The curved *nihonto* (samurai sword) has one of the strongest and most beautiful blades in the world.

Paper Arts

The Japanese have been making paper for thousands of years, using both rice and wood fibers. Their fine handmade paper makes an excellent base for woodblock prints, calligraphy, and ink paintings. It's also sturdy enough for household doors and walls. Each papermaking region specializes in a certain pattern, color, or style of paper.

The people of Gifu are known for their exquisite paper umbrellas, fans, and lanterns.

Children learn origami at home and in school. Paper folding teaches them to use their hands in a precise way and to work with geometric shapes. Birds, fish, frogs, and helmets are some of the basic origami patterns. Experts can make origami kites, fierce masks, and other complex forms.

Kites for Every Occasion

Kite-flying was a popular court activity in the eighteenth century. Fluttering kites (*tako*) were sent aloft as prayers for good luck, thanksgiving, protection from evil, or a child's health. Miniature kites were made of tissue paper on a broom-straw frame and flown on a thread.

"Clam kites" were fun toys for grown-ups. Adults placed a tiny kite inside a clamshell and set the shell on hot coals. In a minute or two, the shell burst open, and the kite shot into the air.

Today, people fly kites on festival days and special occasions. These kites are made of handmade paper stretched over a bamboo frame. Many kite designs have been passed down for generations. They come in an amazing variety of shapes—birds, fish, butterflies, dragonflies, geometric figures, alphabet characters, and even warrior heroes. Some are designed to make humming, whistling, roaring, or screaming sounds.

A kite festival in Shirone

Literature

Court ladies in the Heian period were excellent writers. They developed Japan's hiragana script for writing their diaries, personal memoirs, poetry, and tales. Lady Murasaki Shikibu lived at the emperor's court after her husband died. There she wrote *Genji Monogatari (The Tale of Genji)*, considered the world's first novel. In fifty-four chapters, it recounts the loves and adventures of a handsome young noble. Around the same time, Lady Sei Shonagon wrote *Makura-no-soshi (The Pillow Book)*, a witty report of daily court life.

Japan's first collection of poetry, *Man'yoshu (Collection of 10,000 Leaves)*, dates from the eighth century. By that time, the *tanka*, or *waka*, was the most popular form of poetry. A tanka has five lines, with thirty-one syllables (5, 7, 5, 7, 7). Some Japanese poets still use that form today.

Haiku poems developed in the Edo period, and poets still write them today. A haiku is a three-line poem with seventeen

The Wandering Poet

Matsuo Basho (1644–1694) was a master of the haiku. He took the name Basho, meaning "banana tree," when he moved into a hut beside a banana tree. After studying Zen for many years, Basho took a long journey across Japan. He wrote down his impressions of all that he saw in the form of haiku poetry. Basho taught that the haiku should "seem light as a shallow river flowing over its sandy bed." In Japanese, this famous haiku by Basho has the traditional number of syllables. The English translation has fewer.

> An old pond,
> a frog jumps in—
> a splash of water.

Japanese Proverbs

Proverb	Meaning
A frog in a well doesn't know the ocean.	Someone who lives in a small world doesn't know about the larger world.
Poke a bush, and a snake comes out.	If you go looking for trouble, you will find it.
Even monkeys fall from trees.	Anyone can make a mistake. Or, don't get too proud.
The fallen blossom doesn't return to the branch.	What's done is done.

syllables (5, 7, 5). It uses an image from nature to express a truth about life. At least one key word in the haiku indicates a season of the year. Some of the greatest haiku masters were Basho, Issa, and Buson.

Heroic war tales and dramatic plays were common in medieval times. Professional storytellers memorized thousands of lines of epic poems and recited them as a court entertainment. After a middle class arose in the seventeenth century, the heroes of stories were often common people.

In 1968, Yasunari Kawabata became the first Japanese writer to win the Nobel Prize for Literature. *Snow Country, The Izu Dancer,* and many of his other novels have been translated into other languages. Novelist Kenzaburo Oe won the Nobel Prize in 1994. *The Silent Cry* and *A Personal Matter* are among his best-known novels.

Manga are cartoon stories published as comic books or magazines. Some continue from one issue to the next, for weeks or even years. Manga are popular among both adults and children in many Asian and Western countries.

Comic books called *manga* are very popular in Japan.

Akira Kurosawa

Film director Akira Kurosawa was born in Tokyo in 1910. Western audiences discovered him when *Rashomon* (1950) won the Grand Prize at the Venice Film Festival. Most of Kurosawa's popular samurai films star actor Toshiro Mifune. Kurosawa's 1954 film *The Seven Samurai* depicts Japanese village life in the sixteenth century. Hollywood's *The Magnificent Seven* retells the tale in a Mexican setting. The story line of Kurosawa's *Yojimbo* (1961) shows up in *A Fistful of Dollars*. Even George Lucas's *Star Wars* uses elements from the plot of Kurosawa's *The Hidden Fortress*.

Inset, above: **Posters in English advertise Japan's ever-popular Godzilla movies.**

Giants of the Silver Screen

Akira Kurosawa is Japan's best-known filmmaker. His samurai films are popular all over the world. Many directors have copied Kurosawa's film techniques and story lines. Two other Japanese film masters are Yasujiro Ozu (*Tokyo Story*) and Kenji Mizoguchi (*Ugetsu*).

No one makes monster movies like the Japanese. Godzilla, breathing deadly atomic blasts, first appeared in 1954. Since then, more than twenty Godzilla movies have terrified fans worldwide. Other Japanese monster-movie favorites are Mothra (a giant insect), Rodan (a pterodactyl), Gamera (a fire-spitting turtle), and Gorgo (a mother dinosaur).

Anime are Japanese animated films. Some anime are action-adventure thrillers featuring mythical or ultramodern superheroes. Fans can see their anime champions in videos, video games, and TV shows.

Sumo—An Ancient Tradition

Sumo wrestling is Japan's national sport. Grounded in ancient Shinto myths and rituals, sumo took its present form during the Edo period. Today, more than 500,000 people in Japan belong to sumo clubs.

Sumo wrestlers (*rikishi*) are enormous men weighing 300 pounds (136 kg) or more. They live in the "stable" (*heya*) of a master, where their training is strict and tough. Only a few dozen reach the highest professional levels. They compete in six championship tournaments (*basho*) a year. Few wrestlers ever attain the highest rank of *yokozuna* (grand champion).

Wrestlers style their hair in a topknot and wear a loincloth around their hips. They face off in a circular ring of hand-packed clay measuring 14 feet 9 inches (4.5 m) across. Among the seventy sumo techniques are pushing, slapping, and tripping. The loser is the first to touch outside the ring or to touch the floor with anything besides his feet. In sumo, the mental battle is more important than the physical one. Once the opponents make contact, the match may be over in just a few seconds.

Akebono: Sumo Grand Champion

Taro Akebono (right) is the first non-Japanese to attain the rank of *yokozuna* (grand champion), sumo's highest honor. The 475-pound (215-kg) wrestler was born in Hawaii in 1969 as Chad Rowan. He played basketball in high school and at 18 moved to Japan and began studying sumo. Many said that the 6-foot 8-inch (2-m) wrestler was too tall to succeed at sumo, but he reached the top rank after only five years in the sport. In 1993, he became sumo's sixty-fourth yokozuna. Before that, no one believed it was possible for a *gaijin* (foreigner) to become yokozuna. His success encouraged many other non-Japanese to try the sport. By 1997, Akebono had won nine national championships (*yusho*). He speaks Japanese fluently and became a Japanese citizen in 1996.

A female brown-belt karate expert

Many of Japan's martial arts are combat traditions from the days of the samurai. *Kendo* (the way of the sword) began in the Ashikaga period. The players wear a mask, breastplate, and gloves. Their weapon is a bamboo sword *(shinai)*. Another form of swordsmanship is *iaido*, a lightning-quick sword routine.

Kyudo—traditional Japanese archery—is one of Japan's oldest martial arts. Schools and gyms have kyudo clubs, as do many temples and shrines. Kyudo is an exercise in Zen principles—the ritual movements are more important than hitting the target. Horseback kyudo *(yabasume)* is a Shinto rite involving costumed horsemen.

Jujutsu, or *jujitsu*, arose in the Edo period. This martial art teaches ways of disabling an opponent with quick attacks to the elbow, wrist, and shoulder joints. *Judo* was developed from jujutsu in the 1880s. Opponents grapple using various strangles, locks, and holds. They also use some sumo throwing methods. Judo has been included in the Olympic Games since 1964.

Aikido, developed as recently as the 1920s, uses many jujutsu and judo techniques. The student also learns to use spiritual energy to remain calm, break the opponent's spirit, and predict moves. As in judo, a practitioner lets the attacker's own momentum carry him or her into a fall.

Karate (empty hand) came from China and was refined in Okinawa. Opponents use aggressive punches, jabs, chops, claws, and kicks. Some students condition their hands to chop wood or bricks in one blow. In combat, such a hand could break through armor.

Recreational Sports

Soccer and baseball are the unofficial national sports. Most schools include soccer in their gym programs, and kids love to play it after school. Japan's professional soccer league started its first season in 1993. More than 4 million spectators turned out for the debut.

Baseball is wildly popular. Japan formed its first professional league in 1936. Now there are two leagues—the Central and the Pacific—with six teams each. The two league champions face off every October in the Japan Series, a best-of-seven match. Twice a year, high-school baseball tournaments are held in Hanshin Koshien Stadium in Nishinomiya. Like the pro games, they are major events with intense media coverage.

An English merchant brought golf to Japan in 1901. Today, millions of Japanese men and women enjoy golfing. Businesspeople often plan their business deals on the golf course. Because open land is so scarce, most golf courses are private and very expensive.

In the winter, Japan's snowy mountain resorts are packed with skiers. Other popular sports are tennis, bowling, volleyball, badminton, and swimming.

Japanese athletes first took part in the Olympic Games in 1912 in Stockholm, Sweden. When Tokyo hosted the 1964 Summer Olympics, it was the first time the Olympics were held in Asia. Sapporo hosted the 1972 Winter Olympics, and Nagano hosted the 1998 Winter Olympics. Japan also takes part in the international Asian Games and the Universiade.

Everyday Life in a Changing Society

In conversation, the Japanese try to be gracious. Exploding with anger or irritation is considered uncivilized. If they have a negative or opposing opinion, they say it in a kind, indirect way. Sometimes, *no* is expressed so politely that foreigners might interpret it as *yes*.

116

WHEN JAPANESE PEOPLE MEET, THEY BOW INSTEAD OF SHAKING hands. The lowest bow shows the deepest respect. In business situations, people exchange cards after bowing. Each person examines the card and treats it with respect. Even foreign visitors should present a name card.

Gift-giving is a common social ritual in Japan. A dinner guest presents a wrapped gift to the host. Traditionally, the receiver doesn't unwrap it in the giver's presence. The giver presents the gift humbly, as if it has little value. The receiver responds humbly, too—first declaring that the guest should not have brought a gift, then finally accepting graciously.

Opposite: **A crowded street in Osaka**

A living room with a tatami floor covering and an elegant silk kimono displayed on the wall

Japanese Houses

A traditional Japanese home is wooden with a tile roof. Just inside the front door is the *genkan* (entryway). People remove their shoes there to avoid tracking dirt into the house.

The large front room is for entertaining guests. It's elegantly decorated and may display a prized piece of art. *Tatami*, or straw mats, cover the floors. Large cush-

ions take the place of couches and chairs. Walls are sliding panels of rice paper in wood frames. Sliding the panels can make a room larger or smaller or provide privacy.

The back of the house is the family's living quarters, which include the kitchen, eating and sleeping areas, and the bathroom. At mealtimes, people sit around the table at floor level. Their feet may rest in a sunken area below the table, where heaters warm their feet. Beds are thick cotton mattresses called *futons*. In the morning, the futons are rolled up and put away.

Since World War II, more people live in apartment buildings. Today, many people choose to have Western-style living rooms, dining rooms, and bedrooms, too. But they often keep one tatami room—and the no-shoes rule still applies.

Clothing

Most young people wear uniforms to school. At other times, they relax in jeans, T-shirts, or sweatsuits. For business, men wear conservative suits, and women wear dresses, suits, or skirts and blouses. In some companies, the workers wear company uniforms. For formal ceremonies, men wear a traditional outfit of loose, pleated pants (*hakama*) and a wide-sleeved coat (*haori*).

Kimonos were once everyday clothing for all Japanese. Farmers wore loose work pants over their kimonos. Today, women and girls wear these colorful, wide-sleeved robes on special occasions and festival days. A kimono is made from a long piece of cloth 14 inches (36 cm) wide and painted in bright colors or embroidered. The cloth is cut into eight rectangular panels that are sewn together.

The Japanese eat with chopsticks. Children as young as two or three may start learning to use chopsticks. This custom helps develop their manual skills.

Most meals include rice. The Japanese prefer "sticky rice" rather than the loose rice eaten in China and other countries. Noodles come in many styles. *Udon* (soft, fat wheat noodles), *somen* (very thin noodles), and *soba* (buckwheat noodles) are often served in soups.

Miso soup, served mainly at breakfast, is a soybean and grain broth. Often, fish, seaweed, dried mushroom, or little squares of *tofu*, or soybean curd, are added. The broth is sipped from the bowl, and the solid ingredients are eaten with chopsticks.

The Japanese eat one-sixth of the world's seafood catch. It may be broiled, stewed, or served as *sashimi* or *sushi*. Sashimi is thin slices of raw fish. Sushi may include raw seafood such as salmon, tuna, abalone, or shrimp served on molded, vinegar-flavored rice patties. It's dipped in soy sauce with a pinch of *wasabi* (horseradish paste). Sushi is also prepared in long rolls wrapped in seaweed and cut into slices.

Chopstick Lore

Spread your index finger and thumb apart. Measure the distance between the tip of your index finger and thumb. The perfect chopstick is one-and-a-half times as long as that measurement. Chopsticks should not be licked, waved in the air, left in a rice dish, or used to stab the food.

The Japanese have a saying: "He's never picked up anything heavier than chopsticks." It refers to a wealthy person who has never done any hard work. "Even stumbling chopsticks are funny" is said about people who will laugh at anything.

Everyday Life in a Changing Society   **119**

Typical Japanese Meals

A typical Japanese breakfast consists of rice, miso soup, eggs, grilled fish, dried seaweed, and pickled plums or vegetables. Lunches are light, often consisting of noodles, a sandwich, or *domburi mono* (a bowl of rice with vegetables, meat, or eggs on top). Workers can grab a quick lunch at noodle shops or fast-food stalls.

Dinner is the main meal of the day. In some restaurants, a hot, wet towel is offered before the meal for wiping the hands. Besides rice and clear soup, several fish, meat, or vegetable courses are served. Japanese green tea is offered at the end of the meal.

Eating meat was once discouraged for religious reasons, but many of Japan's standard dishes now include meat. *Sukiyaki* is thin slices of meat with vegetables, noodles, and tofu. *Yakitori* is grilled seafood or meat and vegetables on a skewer. *Shabu-shabu* is boiled slices of meat and vegetables dipped in a sauce.

Food Glossary

breakfast	*asa-gohan*	rice wine	*sake*
dinner	*ban-gohan*	raw fish	*sashimi*
chopsticks	*hashi*	soy sauce	*shoyu*
sushi rolls	*makizushi*	raw fish or other foods with rice	*sushi*
soybean and grain broth	*miso*		
a kind of seaweed	*nori*	eel	*unagi*
fish-cake stew	*oden*	horseradish paste	*wasabi*

Vegetables are served fresh, steamed, pickled, or deep-fried. Some are cut into fancy shapes to decorate a plate. Daikon radishes are cut into a flower shape or a "fisherman's net" pattern, and thin-sliced cucumbers are spread out in a fan shape. *Tempura*—seafood or vegetables covered with batter and deep-fried—dates from the sixteenth century, when Portuguese and Dutch traders introduced fried foods to Japan.

Family Life

Before World War II, three or four generations of a family lived in the same home. Since then, family life has changed dramatically. Now, most Japanese households consist of only parents and their children.

Families are smaller today, too. The average couple has just one or two children. Many couples still take in their elderly parents, but more older people are now living alone. Grown children used to live at home, even after they were married. The trend now is to live in a city apartment or, in some cases, a company dormitory.

Health Benefits of Tea

The monk Eisai wrote, "Tea is a miraculous medicine for the maintenance of health. Tea has an extraordinary power to prolong life." Japanese green tea *(cha)* is known to lower blood pressure, cholesterol, and blood sugar. Some researchers suggest that it also slows the aging process, prevents cavities, and fights viruses.

Families enjoying Disneyland in suburban Tokyo

Getting Married in Japan

A bride goes through several "costumes" on her wedding day. For the Shinto wedding ceremony, she wears a white kimono, signifying her purity. In rural areas, the white-clad bride sits on display in her home for all the neighbors to see before the wedding.

The Shinto ritual itself is short. First the priest purifies the couple and prays for the gods' blessings. Then they sip sake from three cups and exchange marriage vows.

At the reception, the bride arrives in a multicolored kimono. After guests give speeches and toasts, the bride changes into a Western-style white wedding gown and veil. Next comes an elaborate party dress. The groom changes from a ceremonial robe with loose-fitting pants to a tuxedo or suit. All of these customs are patterned after Crown Prince Yoshihito's wedding in 1900.

"Love matches" (marriages between two people who meet and fall in love) are becoming more common, especially in urban areas. But traditional arranged marriages prevail even among modern young professionals. Relatives, matchmakers, or marriage bureaus introduce the couple. After three or four meetings, it's assumed that they're seriously interested in each other. However, either party can "back out" at any point in the process.

Changing Roles for Women

Women became the legal equals of men in Japan in 1947. However, most women still follow the traditional roles of wife, mother, and homemaker. Working women usually quit their jobs when they get married or when they have their first baby.

Even though tradition still holds, some Japanese women are forging new roles for themselves. More married women are keeping their jobs or finding new ones, taking college courses, and doing volunteer work. Single working women enjoy the freedom of having their own money to spend. They shop for designer clothes, go to discos, and take overseas trips. Once they're married, they tone down their makeup and wear more conservative clothes.

Young women are marrying later than their mothers did. In 1990, the average Japanese woman married at twenty-six, compared to age twenty-three in 1947. In a recent survey, 40 percent of single women said they would choose not to marry if they could afford it.

Young people relax at a virtual-reality theme park.

Growing Up in Japan

Children in Japan enjoy many of the same pastimes as young people in other countries. They like playing soccer, playing video games, playing cards, reading comic books, listening to music, and talking on the phone. They ride bikes and unicycles, swim, and fly kites. Younger children like to watch superhero cartoons. Many young people take piano or violin lessons after school. Some teenagers work at part-time jobs to earn money to buy the latest fashions and CDs.

Japan has its share of young rebels. Every Sunday, a very un-Japanese ritual takes place in Tokyo's Yoyogi Park. Thousands of teenagers show up in both nostalgic and current Western-style dress. They play loud music, dance in the streets, and eat Western junk food.

Every Sunday, teenagers dressed as Western rock stars of the 1950s come to Tokyo's Yoyogi Park to sing and dance.

To older people, this behavior is not very upsetting. They feel sure that the teenagers will "get straight" once they get jobs and get married. Usually, the older people are right. Jeans give way to suits and dresses, and soft drinks are replaced by coffee or tea.

A "Growing" Population

In the 1850s, the average height of a Japanese man was 5 feet 3 inches (160 cm). Women averaged 4 feet 10 inches (147 cm). With more protein in their diet, the Japanese have grown taller. Today, Japanese men average about 5 feet 9 inches (175 cm) tall, and women, 5 feet 3 inches (160 cm). Today's teenagers will be even taller as adults.

Dancers perform a traditional dragon dance in the New Year parade in Yokohama's Chinatown.

Every week of the year, somewhere in Japan, a festival is going on. Some are religious, such as the matsuri, or Shinto shrine festivals. Others honor historical people or events. Most religious feast days are set by the lunar calendar, which follows the cycles of the moon, so they fall on different days every year. Other holidays, such as New Year's, always occur on the same date.

Shogatsu, or New Year's, is the biggest celebration of the year. Festivities last for several days. Residents clean their homes, and shopkeepers scrub their stores from top to bottom. Everybody wants to start fresh in the new year. Some ladies dress up in kimonos and grand, Edo-period hairstyles. Families gather for a huge feast on New Year's Eve.

At midnight, Buddhist temples toll their bells 108 times, driving out the 108 worldly passions. People gather at shrines to pray for good fortune in the year ahead. At Kyoto's Yasaka Shrine, a sacred fire is lit at midnight. Worshipers take glowing embers from the fire to cook the new year's first meal.

January 15, Coming-of-Age Day, is for twenty-year-olds. It marks the day when they officially become adults. Young men dress in suits, and young women wear beautiful kimonos. They march in a formal parade, and family and friends give them gifts and parties. After that day, they can vote, marry, and make other adult decisions without their parents' consent.

Setsubun, the Bean-Throwing Festival, marks the end of winter. By the lunar calendar, it's usually in early February. Temple priests throw beans to the crowds as everyone chants, "In with good fortune, out with the devils!" Hokkaido's week-long Snow Festival also takes place in early February. In Sapporo, huge sculptures of snow and ice line the main street.

A *hina* doll display

March 3 is the Doll Festival, a special day for girls. They dress in kimonos and display their *hina* dolls—an emperor, empress, and attendants dressed in ancient costume. Buddhist temples all over Japan celebrate Buddha's birthday on April 8.

Everyone tries to go on vacation for "Golden Week"—April 29 through May 5. The cherry blossoms are in bloom, and people turn out for flower-watching and picnics under the trees. May 5 used to be just for boys, but now it's Children's Day. To inspire noble behavior in their children, families display samurai mannequins and armor in their homes. Outside, they fly carp-shaped windsocks that fill with air in the breeze.

National Holidays

January 1	New Year's Day
January 15	Coming-of-Age Day
February 11	National Foundation Day
March 20/21	Spring Equinox
April 29	Greenery Day
May 3	Constitution Memorial Day
May 5	Children's Day (above)
July 20	Marine Day
September 15	Respect-for-the-Aged Day
September 22/23/24	Autumn Equinox
October 10	Health and Sports Day
November 3	Culture Day
November 23	Labor Thanksgiving Day
December 23	Emperor Akihito's Birthday

The Bon Festival takes place on July 13–15 or August 13–15, depending on the location. This is the time when departed spirits are believed to revisit the Earth. People go back to their hometowns to honor their ancestors. As a farewell to the dead, the participants set flickering paper lanterns afloat on the waters.

Mid-September brings the shrine festival at Tsurugaoka Hachimangu Shrine in Kamakura. It ends with a dashing display of yabasume, or horseback archery.

November 15 is *Shichi-go-san* (Seven-five-three), a Shinto festival for children. They dress in their best clothes and visit favorite shrines. There they give thanks for being alive and pray for future health and good fortune. Children who are seven, five, and three years old get special notice.

More than 2,000 costumed people march in the *Jidai Matsuri* at Kyoto's Heian Shrine. The matsuri at Kyoto's Yasaka Shrine lasts the entire month of July. Countless other shrine festivals take place throughout the year. Many draw great crowds to see their processions, floats, dances, plays, fireworks, and bonfires.

Any day is a good day for *pachinko,* a popular pinball game played on an upright board. Its name comes from *pa-ching!*—the sound a pinball makes when it's fired. Only adults are allowed in pachinko parlors.

Some of Japan's tabletop games are hundreds of years old. *Shogi* is a board game similar to chess. The object is to capture the other player's king. *Sugoroku* is a Japanese version of Parcheesi. *Go* is a board game that the Japanese have been playing since the eighth century.

Karaoke means "empty orchestra." That's a good name for this popular entertainment. The empty orchestra is a music-only tape that backs up amateur crooners. Karaoke began in Japanese nightclubs in the early 1970s. It quickly spread throughout Japan and caught on in the United States. Karaoke bars are favorite after-work hangouts.

On their days off, people like to spend the day in the countryside or go hiking in the mountains. On weekends, they may take off for hot mineral springs, health spas, or amusement parks. Cherry blossom season finds them picnicking under the trees.

Leisure time is a fairly new discovery for the Japanese people. Some welcome the chance to develop hobbies such as painting, while others visit famous shrines. Many just want to spend more time with their families. Hard work built Japan into one of the world's wealthiest nations. Now the Japanese people are using their hard-earned leisure to pursue a richer quality of life.

Let's Play Go!

The go board is a grid with nineteen horizontal and nineteen vertical lines, making 361 intersections. One player begins with 181 black stones, and the other gets 180 white stones. One by one, each player places a stone on an intersection. The object is to build lines of stones that surround the other player's pieces. Surrounded stones are then "dead." After all the stones are on the board, the player who has captured more of the other player's stones is the winner.

Timeline

c. 2500 B.C. Egyptians build the Pyramids
and Sphinx in Giza.

Japan History

Jimmu Tenno becomes ruler of Japan. **1st century** A.D.

563 B.C. The Buddha is born in India.

A.D. 313 The Roman emperor Constantine
recognizes Christianity.

The Yamato clan becomes the most A.D. 350
powerful clan.

Buddhist scriptures are introduced into 538
Japan.

Empress Suiko reigns. 593 – 628

The seventeen-article constitution 604
is written.

610 The prophet Muhammad begins preaching
a new religion called Islam.

Emperor Kammu reigns. 781 – 806

Emperor Kammu establishes Kyoto as 794
capital of Japan.

1054 The Eastern (Orthodox) and Western
(Roman) churches break apart.

1066 William the Conqueror defeats
the English in the Battle of Hastings.

1095 Pope Urban II proclaims the First Crusade.

Taira family takes political control away 1160
from the Fujiwaras.

Yoritomo is appointed shogun. 1192

Kublai Khan attempts to invade Japan. 1274

1215 King John seals the Magna Carta.

c. 1300 The Renaissance begins in Italy.

1347 The Black Death sweeps through Europe.

1453 Ottoman Turks capture Constantinople,
conquering the Byzantine Empire.

1492 Columbus arrives in North America.

Japan History

The Portuguese arrive in Japan.	**1543**
Francis Xavier introduces Christianity into Japan.	**1549**
Japan invades Korea.	**1592**
Christian priests are forced to leave Japan.	**1614**
Mount Fuji erupts for the last time.	**1707**
U.S. Commodore Matthew C. Perry reaches Japan.	**1853**
Japan and China are at war.	**1894 – 1895**
Korea becomes a Japanese colony.	**1910**
Earthquakes strike Tokyo and Yokohoma.	**1923**
Japan attacks Pearl Harbor, and the United States declares war.	**1941**
Atomic bombs are dropped by the United States on Hiroshima and Nagasaki.	**1945**
U.S. occupation of Japan ends.	**1952**
Okinawa is returned to Japan by the United States.	**1972**
Crown Prince Akihito becomes the 125th emperor of the Chrysanthemum Throne.	**1989**

World History

c. 1500	The Reformation leads to the birth of Protestantism.
1776	The Declaration of Independence is signed.
1789	The French Revolution begins.
1865	The American Civil War ends.
1914	World War I breaks out.
1917	The Bolshevik Revolution brings Communism to Russia.
1929	Worldwide economic depression begins.
1939	World War II begins, following the German invasion of Poland.
1957	The Vietnam War starts.
1989	The Berlin Wall is torn down, as Communism crumbles in Eastern Europe.
1996	Bill Clinton is reelected U.S. president.

Fast Facts

Official Name: *Nippon* or *Nihon* (Japan)

Capital: Tokyo

Kuril Islands

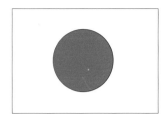

Flag of Japan

Imperial family

Tokyo

Official language:	Japanese	
Official religion:	None	
National anthem:	"Kimigayo" ("The Reign of Our Emperor")	
Government:	Constitutional monarchy with a National Diet consisting of two legislative houses	
Chief of state:	Emperor	
Head of government:	Prime Minister	
Area:	145,870 square miles (377,802 sq km)	
Coordinates of geographic center:	30°00' N, 138°00' E	
Bordering countries:	Japan lies across from Russia, Korea, and China.	
Highest elevation:	Mount Fuji, 12,388 feet (3,776 m)	
Lowest elevation:	Sea level along coasts	

Average temperatures (year-round):

	January	July
Tokyo	46°F (8°C)	82°F (28°C)
Sapporo	28°F (–2°C)	75°F (24°C)

Average annual rainfall: 40 inches (102 cm)

National population: 123,611,167 (1990 census); 126,320,000 (1996 est.)

Population of largest cities (1990 census):

Tokyo	8,163,573
Yokohama	3,220,331
Osaka	2,623,801
Nagoya	2,154,793
Sapporo	1,671,742
Kobe	1,477,410
Kyoto	1,461,103

Himeji-jo Castle

Famous landmarks:
   ▶ *Myohoin Temple* (Kyoto)

   ▶ *Tokyo National Museum*

   ▶ *Himeji-jo Castle* (Himeji, near Kobe)

   ▶ *Matsumoto Castle* (Matsumoto)

Industry: Japan's economy is one of the largest in the world, exceeded only by the United States. The Japanese manufacture an enormous number of goods that are in great demand around the world. These include automobiles, computers, consumer electronics, steel, and textiles. The manufacturing facilities in Japan are among the most modern in the world.

Currency: 1 yen ¥ = 100 sen; 1 U.S.$=¥130 (April 1998)

Weights and measures: Metric

Literacy: Virtually 100%

Common Japanese words and phrases:

hai (HAH-ee)	yes
iie (ee-EH)	no
domo arigato (DOH-moh ah-REE-gah-toh)	thank you
sumimasen (soo-MEE-mah-sehn)	excuse me
ohayo gozaimasu (oh-HAH-yoh goh-ZAH-ee-mahs)	good morning
konnichi wa (KOHN-nee-chee-wah)	good day
oyasumi nasai (oh-YAH-soo-mee nah-sah-ee)	good night
sayonara (sah-YOH-nah-rah)	good-bye

Akira Kurosawa

Famous Japanese:

Kobo Abe Writer	(1924–1993)
Akihito Emperor	(1933–)
Leo Esaki Physicist and Nobel Prize winner	(1925–)
Hirohito Emperor	(1901–1989)
Yasunari Kawabata Writer and Nobel Prize winner	(1899–1972)
Akira Kurosawa Film director	(1910–)
Toshiro Mifune Actor	(1920–1997)
Seiji Ozawa Orchestra conductor	(1935–)
Yasujiro Ozu Film director	(1903–1963)
Kenzo Tange Architect	(1913–)
Hideki Tojo Prime minister	(1884–1948)

To Find Out More

Nonfiction

▶ Brooks, Philip. *Japan*. Danbury, Conn.: Children's Press, 1995.

▶ Bunce, Vincent. *Japan*. Danbury, Conn.: Franklin Watts, 1997.

▶ Galvin, Irene Flum. *Japan: A Modern Land with Ancient Roots*. Tarrytown, N.Y.: Marshall Cavendish, 1996.

▶ Herr, Myra. *Ancient Japan*. Santa Monica, Calif.: Goodyear, 1992. Ross, Stewart.

▶ Ross, Stewart. *Causes and Consequences of the Rise of Japan and the Pacific Rim*. Austin, Tex.: Raintree/Steck-Vaughn, 1995.

▶ Scoones, Simon. *A Family from Japan*. Austin, Tex.: Raintree/Steck-Vaughn, 1998.

▶ Tames, Richard. *Exploration into Japan*. New York: New Discovery, 1995.

▶ Weston, Reiko, Robert L. Wolfe, and Diane Wolfe. *Cooking the Japanese Way*. Minneapolis: Lerner Publications, 1989.

▶ Young, Robert. *Hiroshima: Fifty Years of Debate*. New York: Dillon Press, 1994.

Biography

▶ Blumberg, Rhoda. *Commodore Perry in the Land of the Shogun*. New York: Lothrop, Lee & Shepard, 1985.

Fiction

▶ Brenner, Barbara, and Julia Takaya. *Chibi: A True Story from Japan*. New York: Clarion Books, 1996.

▶ Buck, Pearl S. *The Big Wave*. New York: J. Day, 1948 (also HarperCrest paperback reprint, 1973).

▶ Haugaard, Erik Christian. *The Boy and the Samurai*. Boston: Houghton Mifflin, 1991.

▶ Namioka, Lensey. *Den of the White Fox*. San Diego: Harcourt Brace, 1997.

Folktales

▶ Haviland, Virginia, and Carol Inouye. *Favorite Fairy Tales Told in Japan*. New York: Beech Tree Books, 1996.

▶ Uchida, Yoshiko, and Richard C. Jones. *The Dancing Kettle and Other Japanese Folk Tales*. Berkeley, Calif.: Creative Arts Book Co., 1986.

Websites

▶ **The Embassy of Japan**
http://www.embjapan.org/
The official website of the Japanese Embassy in Washington, D.C.

▶ **Japan Information Network**
http://www.jinjapan.org/
Links to a wide range of information on Japanese history, culture, current events, and government

▶ **Kids Web Japan**
http://www.jinjapan.org/kidsweb/
A site designed specifically for young people, available in seven languages

Organizations and Embassies

▶ **The Asia Society**
Education Department
Educational Programs Division
725 Park Avenue
New York, NY 10021
(212) 288-6400

▶ **Embassy of Japan**
2520 Massachusetts Avenue, N.W.
Washington, DC 20008
(202) 939-6700

Index

Page numbers in *italics* indicate illustrations.

Meet the Author

ANN HEINRICHS FELL IN LOVE WITH FARAWAY PLACES WHILE reading Doctor Dolittle books as a child. She has traveled through most of the United States and several countries in Europe, as well as northwest Africa, the Middle East, and east Asia.

"Trips are fun, but the real work—tracking down all the factual information for a book—begins at the library. I head straight for the reference department. Some of my favorite resources are United Nations publications, world almanacs, and the library's computer databases.

"For this book, I also read several issues of *The Japan Times* and the *Far East Economic Review*. I attended exhibits and lectures on Japanese art, saw a no theater performance, watched *kyudo* (archery) and *aikido* (a martial art) demonstrations, and saw half a dozen Akira Kurosawa movies. I played go, made origami animals, practiced Zen meditation, waitressed in a sushi bar, and ate my weight in sushi. Talking with Japanese people about their country and culture gave me valuable insights, too.

"To me, writing nonfiction is a bigger challenge than writing fiction. With nonfiction, you can't just dream something up—everything has to be researched. When I uncover the facts, they always turn out to be more spectacular than fiction could ever be. And I'm always on the lookout for what kids in another country are up to, so I can report back to kids here."

Ann Heinrichs grew up in Arkansas and lives in Chicago. She is the author of more than twenty-five books for children and young adults on American, Asian, and African history and culture. (*Tibet*, in Children's Press's Enchantment of the World series, was awarded honorable mention by the National Federation of Press Women.)

Ann has also written numerous newspaper, magazine, and encyclopedia articles and critical reviews. As an advertising copywriter, she has covered everything from plumbing hardware to Oriental rugs. She holds a bachelor's and master's degree in piano performance. These days, her performing arts are the martial arts *t'ai chi chuan* and *kung fu* sword.

Photo Credits